Compassionate Eye

Finding Peace

慈眼視衆生

Eyes of compassion
Observing sentient beings
Assemble an ocean
Of blessings
Beyond measure

Lotus Sutra

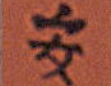

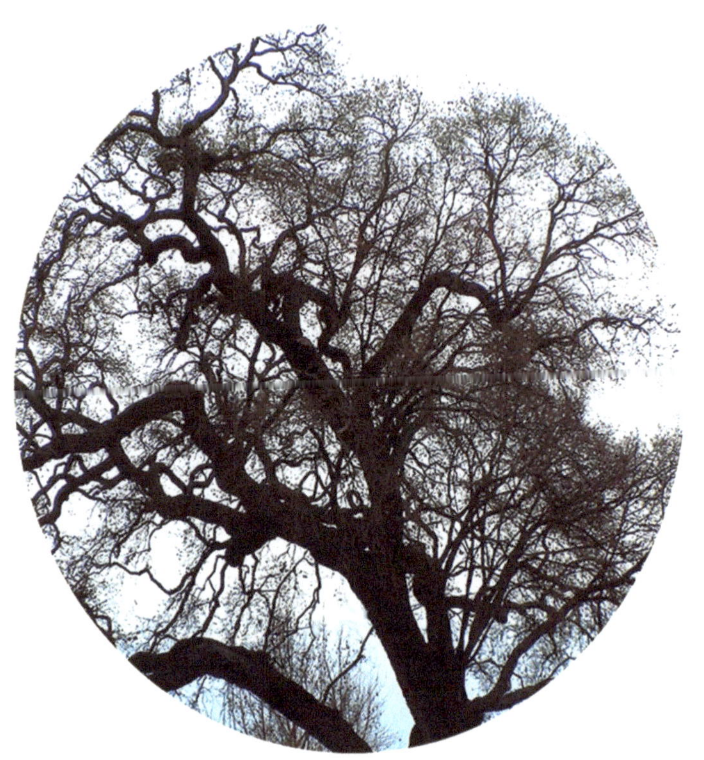

Trees Speak of Love

we have roots
that grow

       one to another

limbs that reach out

       one to another

when all the leaves
fall from our branches
we discover
we are one treee

       all one to another

Photo Credits: Carol Plone, p.40, 52
All Other Photos: @ 2022 Allen Plone
Illustrations: p.50, 60: @ Chip Miller

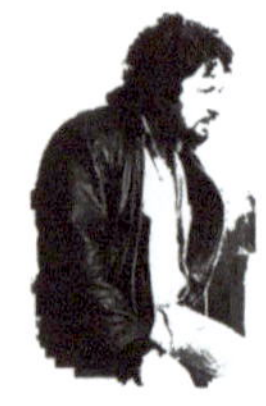

ISBN 878-0-578-29265-6 (paperback)
Library of Congress Control Number 2022909970
Copyright © 2022 Allen Plone

sit in the center of happiness
let it creep up your spine
smear on your face
    a kid tasting jam
    for the first time

let joy bubble through
your mouth in soft spurts
fill in the space
left bare by the everyday

roll in luxury of silence
plump it into a pillow
to rest your head

be a bird escaped
from a cramping cage
holding its song sacred
inside its tight beak
until it feels its wings open
      then
burst into life

spend a moment
wanting only
to be alone
with the sky rain

sun when it returns
from behind a cloud

Preface

What is compassion? It's a way of being that reacts to seeing suffering; in others and in yourself. Compassion begins when we become aware of the simple truth that suffering exists in the world. It progresses to feeling moved by observing suffering, by feeling it. Feeling suffering in self and others evokes the desire to relieve the suffering by taking action to end it. Compassion, then, is the essence of enlightenment. Without compassion, there is no love. Without love, there is no enlightenment. There is no joy.

Buddha teaches that enlightenment comes when we truly cultivate two qualities: wisdom and compassion. Compassion is necessary to temper and better our wisdom. Compassion is the "feeling" side of our nature. It is the ability to feel the suffering of all living beings, from the tiniest to the largest. From the smallest insect to the greatest tree. The truly compassionate person is obliged to take action and help end suffering for all; people, plants, insects and animals. Compassion means taking action to end suffering without the expectation of reward. To put yourself in the place of others, to underestand their suffering, is the true beginning of love. When we understand the suffering of others, we come to better know and understand ourselves. That understanding and the compassion we feel and act upon is the true essence of love.

This book is my journey, upon which I invite you to join, to better understand and embrace compassion. It's failures are my own. It's successes are everyones.

Allen Plone, 2022

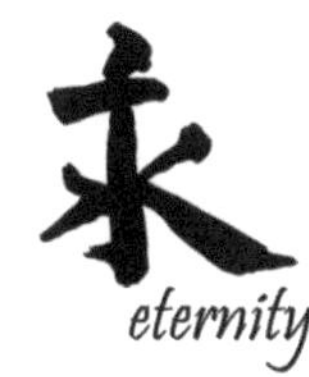

A PRAYER

May all beings everywhere,
with whom we are inseparably
interconnected be fulfilled and free.

May there be peace in this world
and throughout the universe
and may we all together
complete the journey in joy.

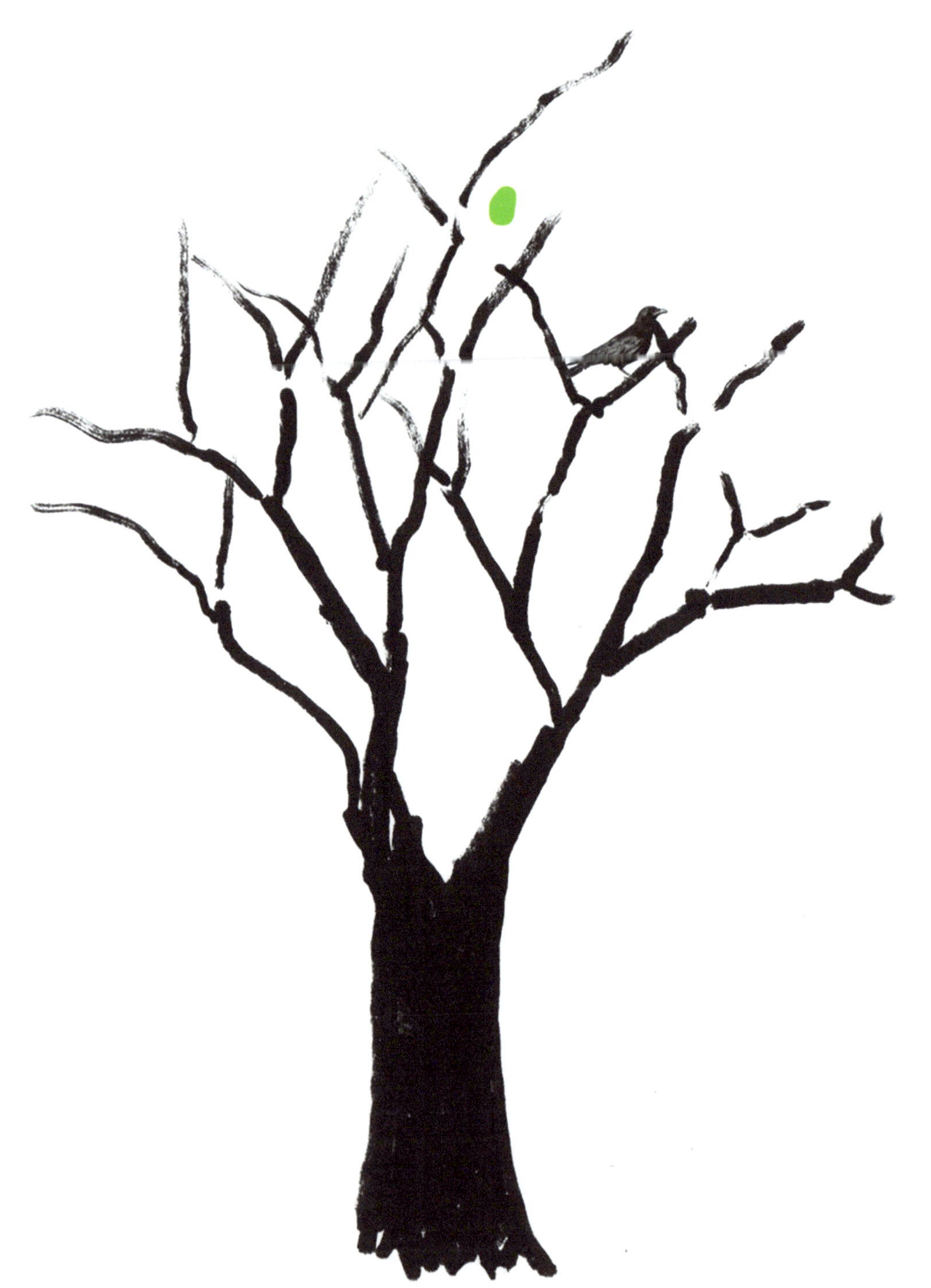

THE SHAPE OF A TREE

the seed it's said
determines the tree
yet the living thing
defies its birth
to become not what it must
but what it will

choice defines its splendor
one from infinite possibilities
unique yet part of the forest

a windless world an impossible constant
the path towards the seed's dream
the hope of perfection foiled

a crown shaped by storm
boughs bent by hungry visits
these are the gifts of being

ask the perched raven
how many lifetimes needed
to see all the world's beauty

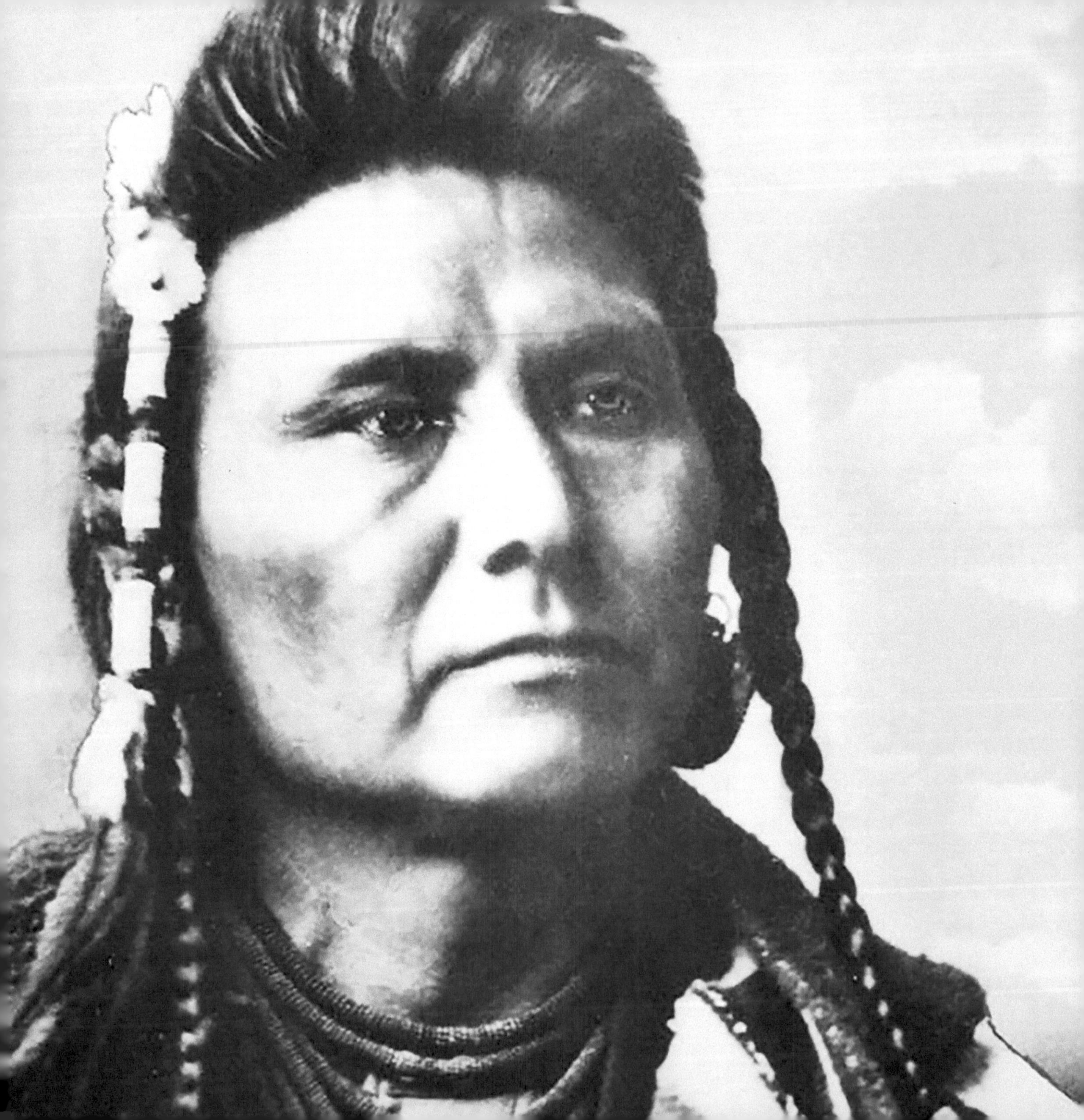

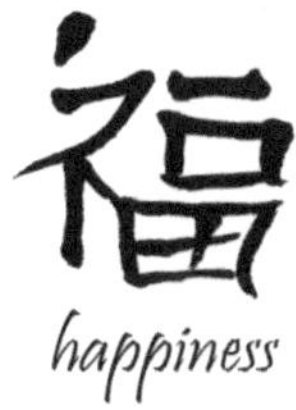

happiness

Eyes of compassion
observing sentient beings
assemble an ocean
of blessings, peace,
happiness beyond measure

Buddha

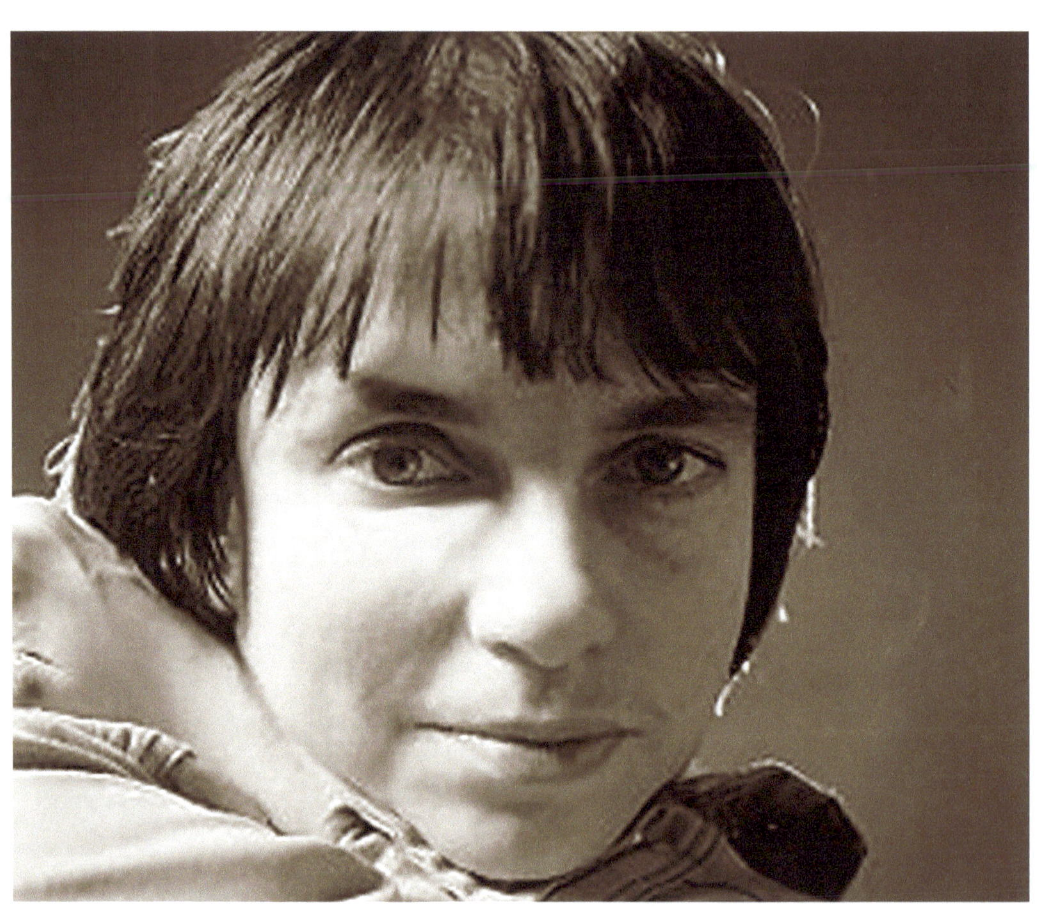

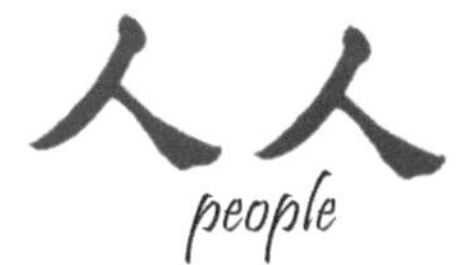

Compassion is the
wish to see others
free from suffering.

The Dalai Lama

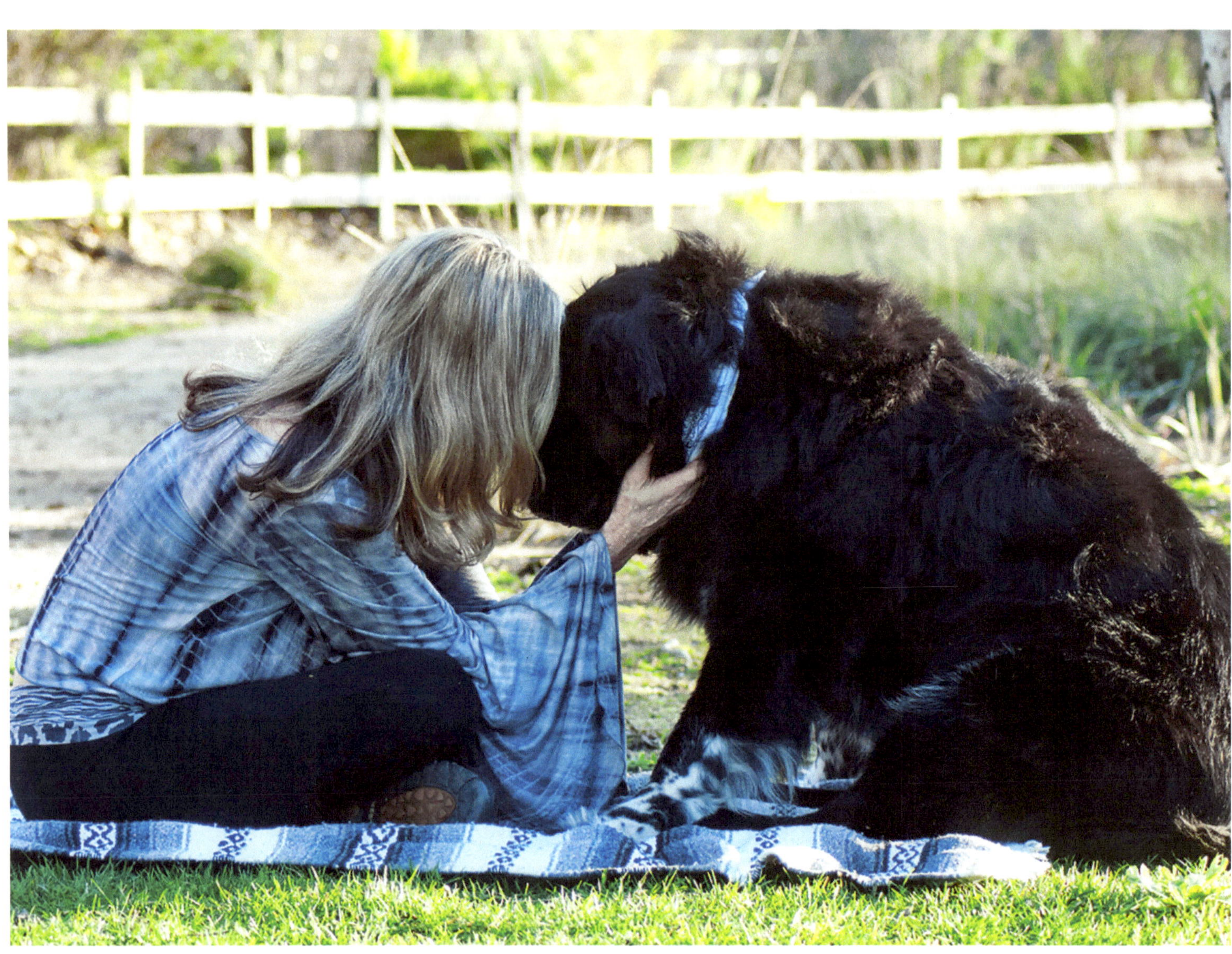

力
strength

Compassion is a muscle
that gets stronger with use.

Ghandi

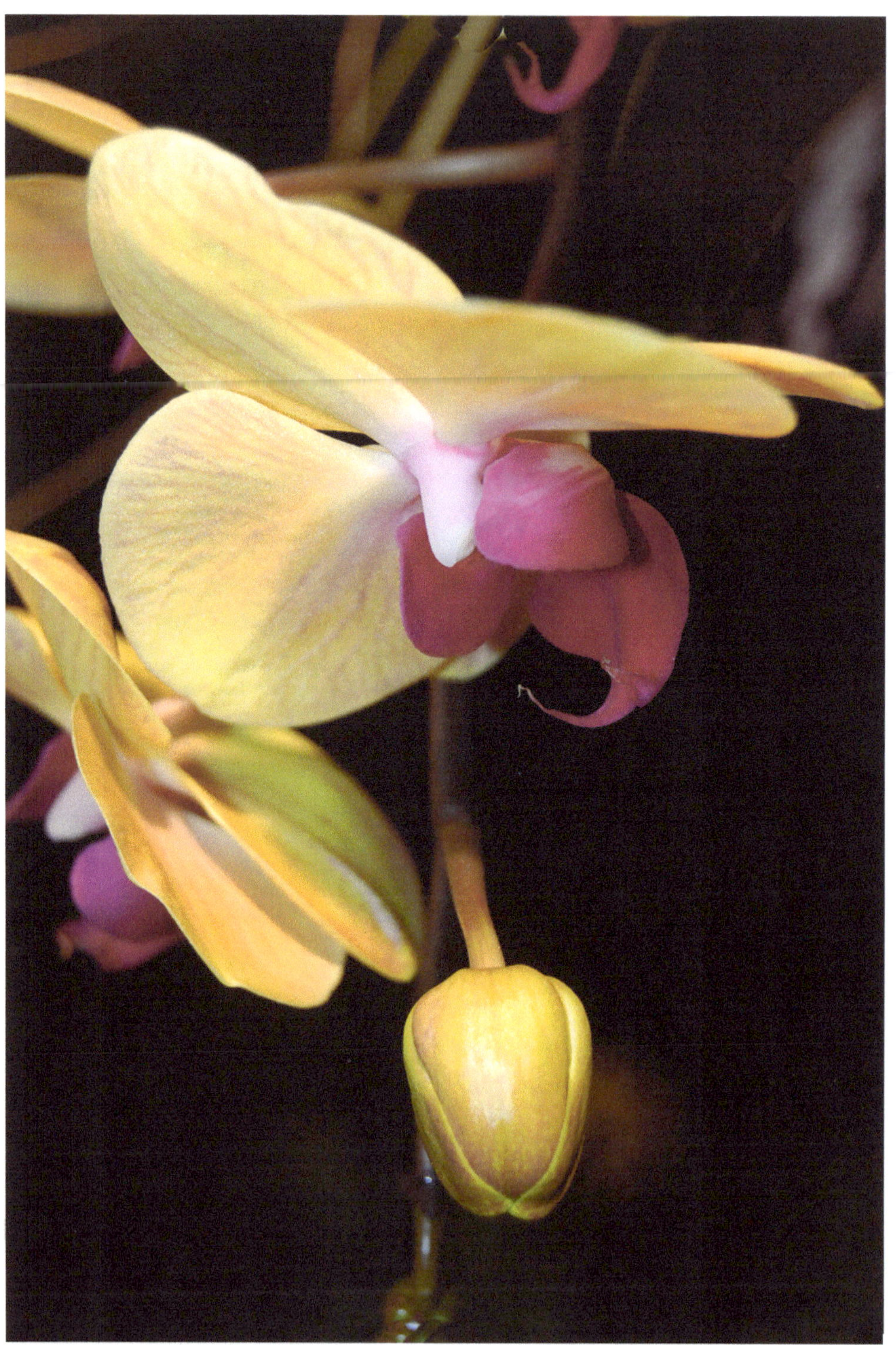

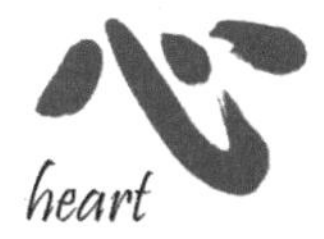

What comes from the heart
touches the heart

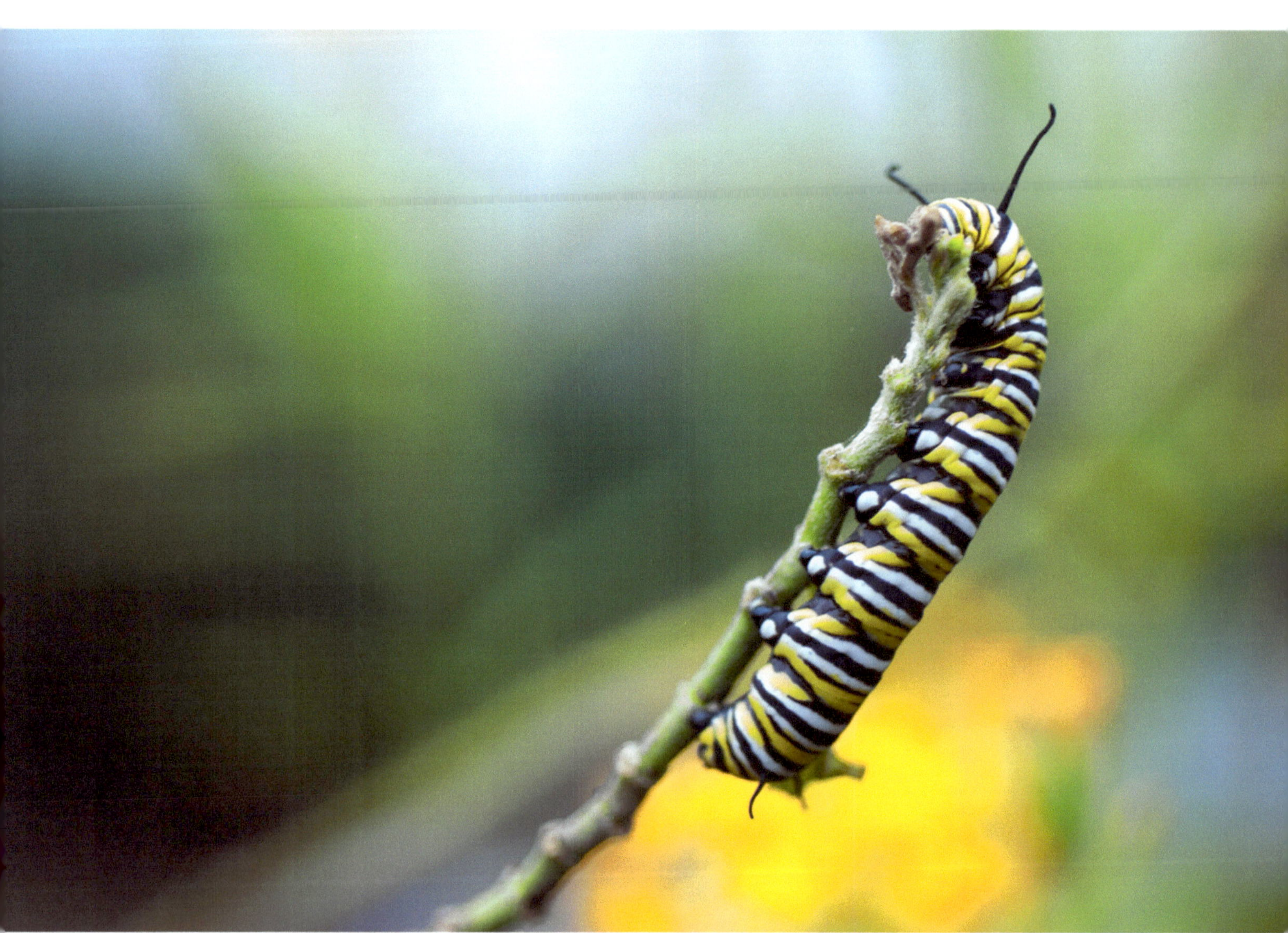

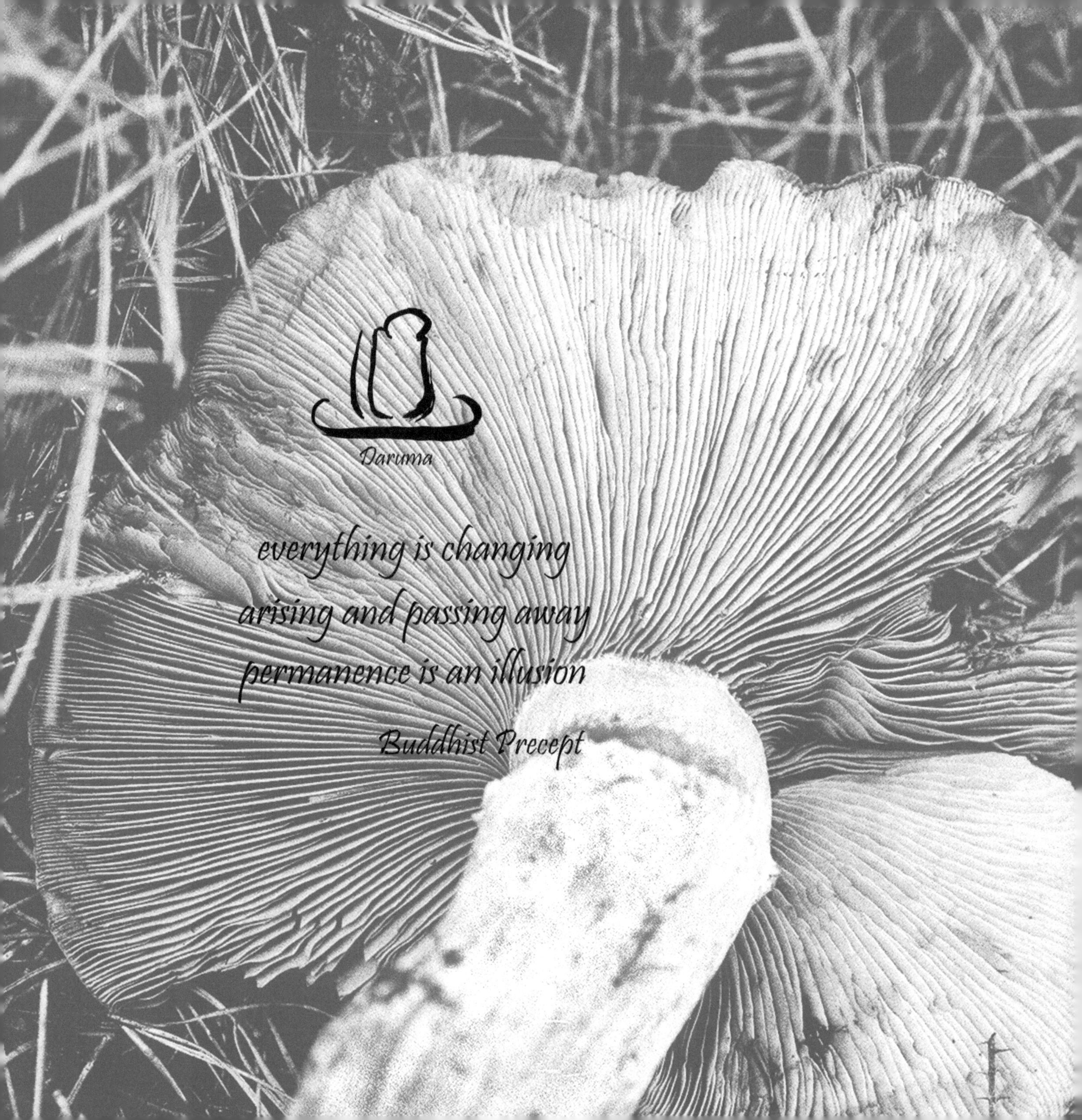

Daruma

everything is changing

arising and passing away

permanence is an illusion

Buddhist Precept

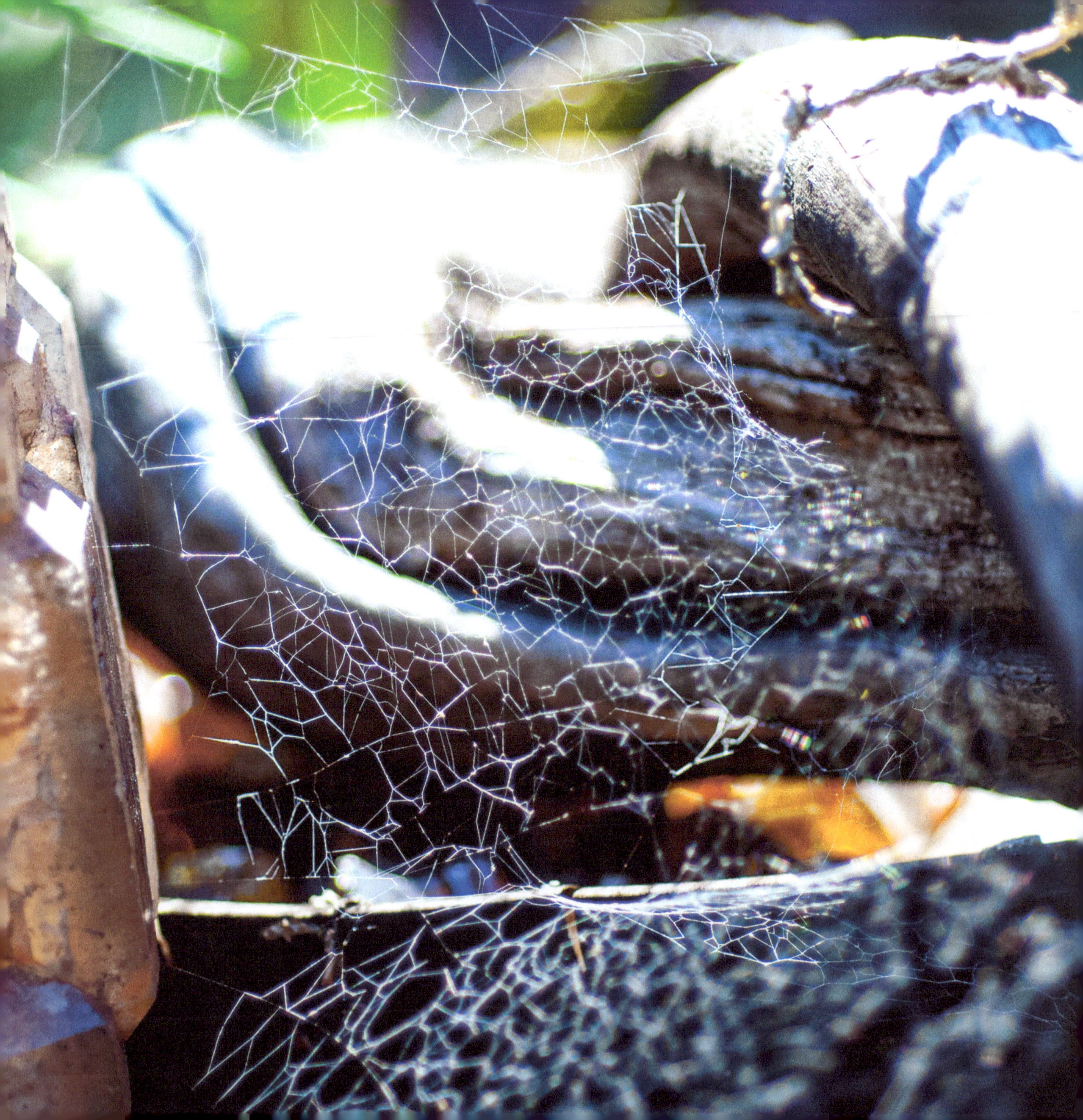

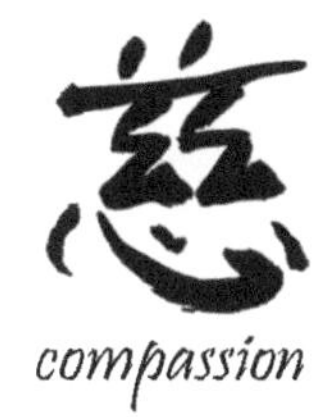

compassion

beyond Maya's illusions
is the reality
of being and consciousness

a self of all things
one and eternal

all beings are united in the one self

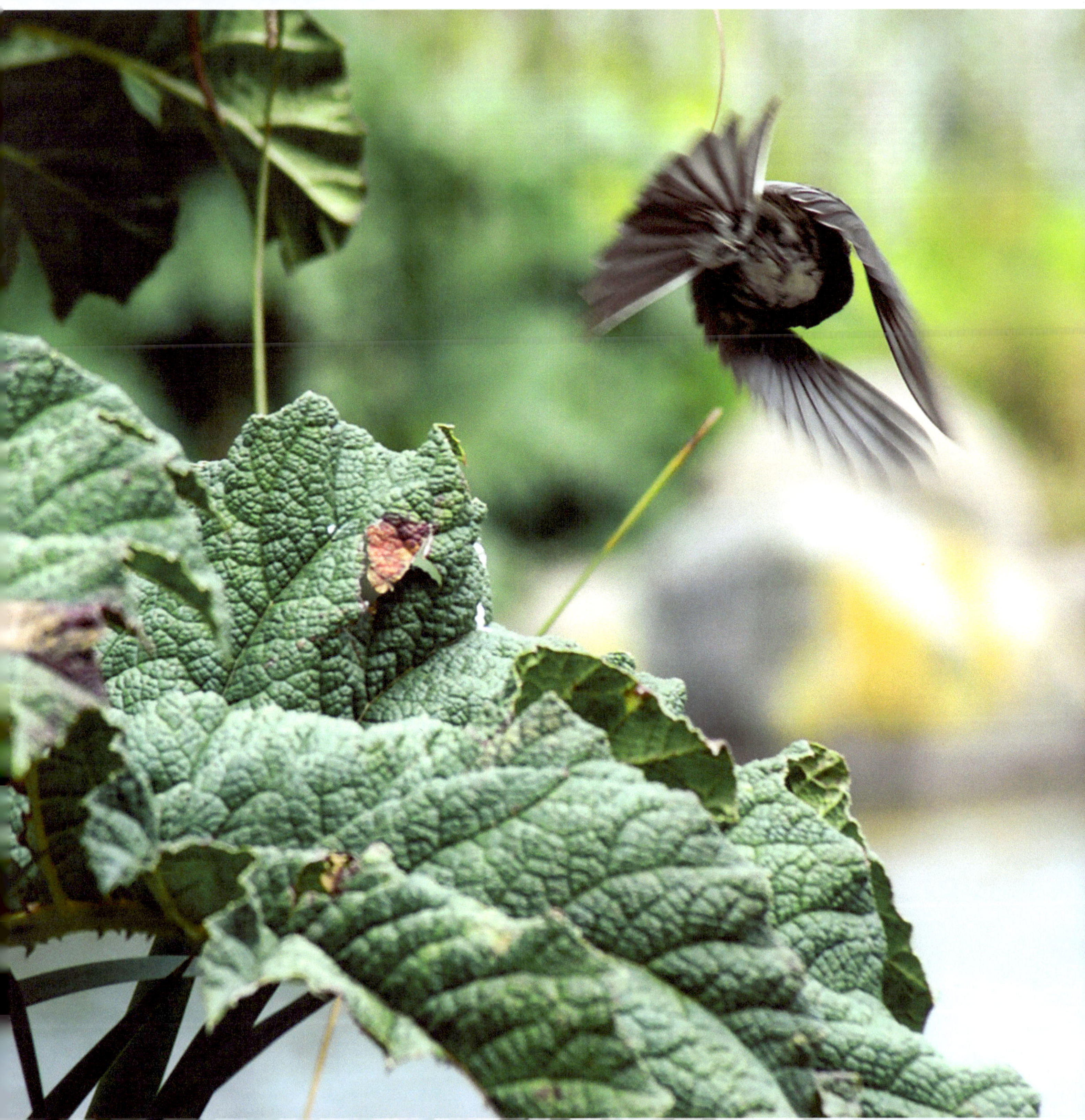

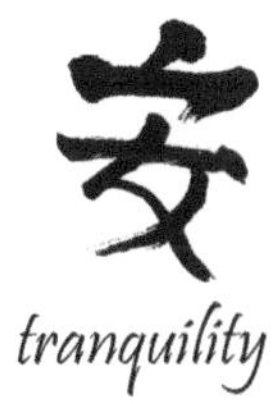

tranquility

*In the morning, I vow with all beings,
to be ready to receive the Dharma
from flowers or children or birds.*

Zen Mantra

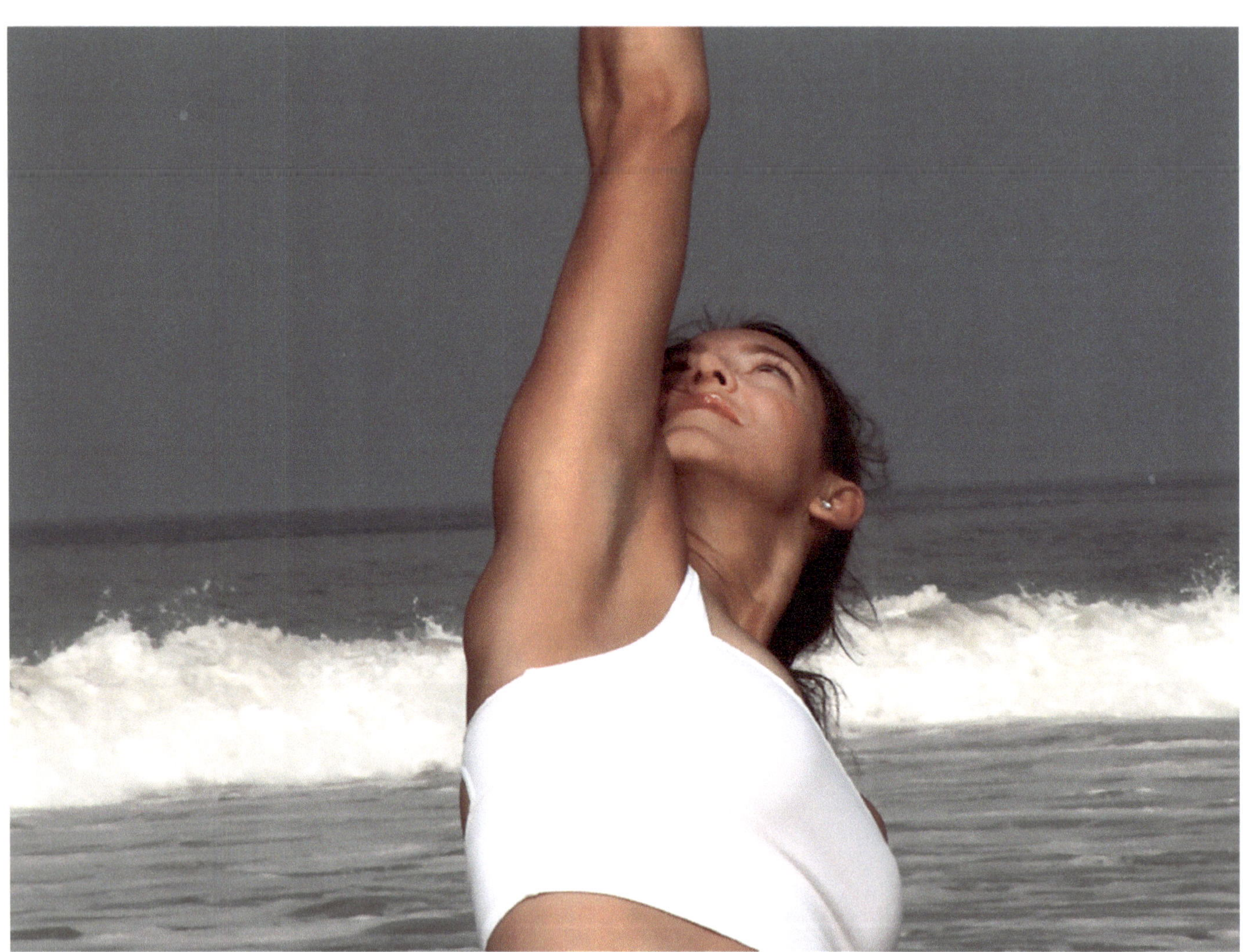

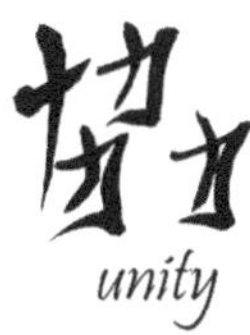

unity

Wisdom appears from a pure and peaceful mind. To walk safely through life, one needs the light of wisdom and the guidance of virtue. The only real failure in life is not to be true to the best one can be.

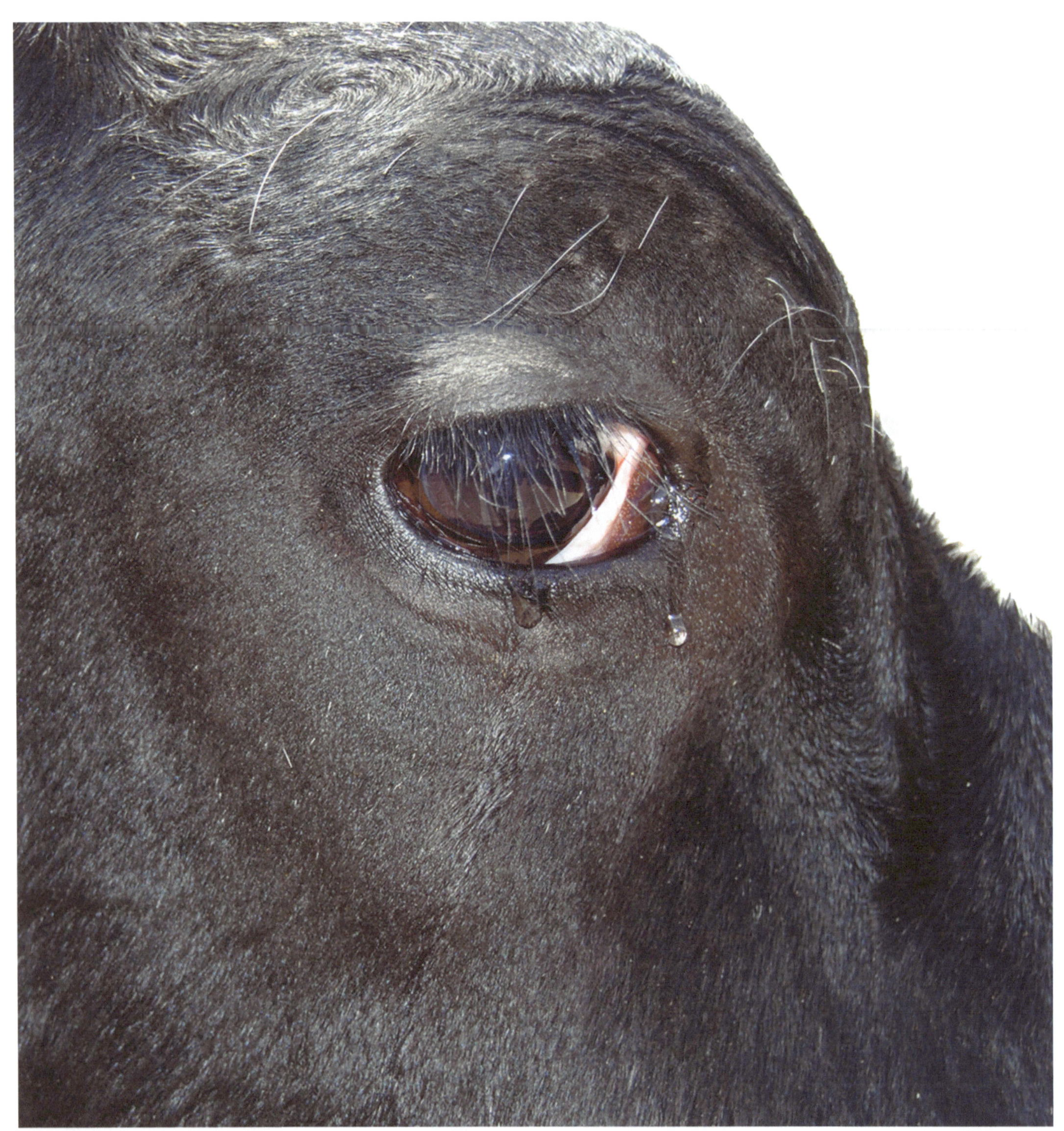

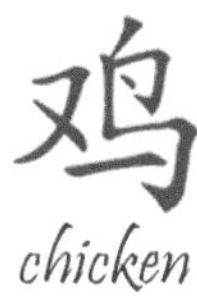

鸡

chicken

The assumption that animals are without rights and the illusion that our treatment of them has no moral significance is a positively outrageous example of Western crudity and barbarity. Universal compassion is the only guarantee of morality.

Arthur Schopenhauer
"The Basis of Morality"

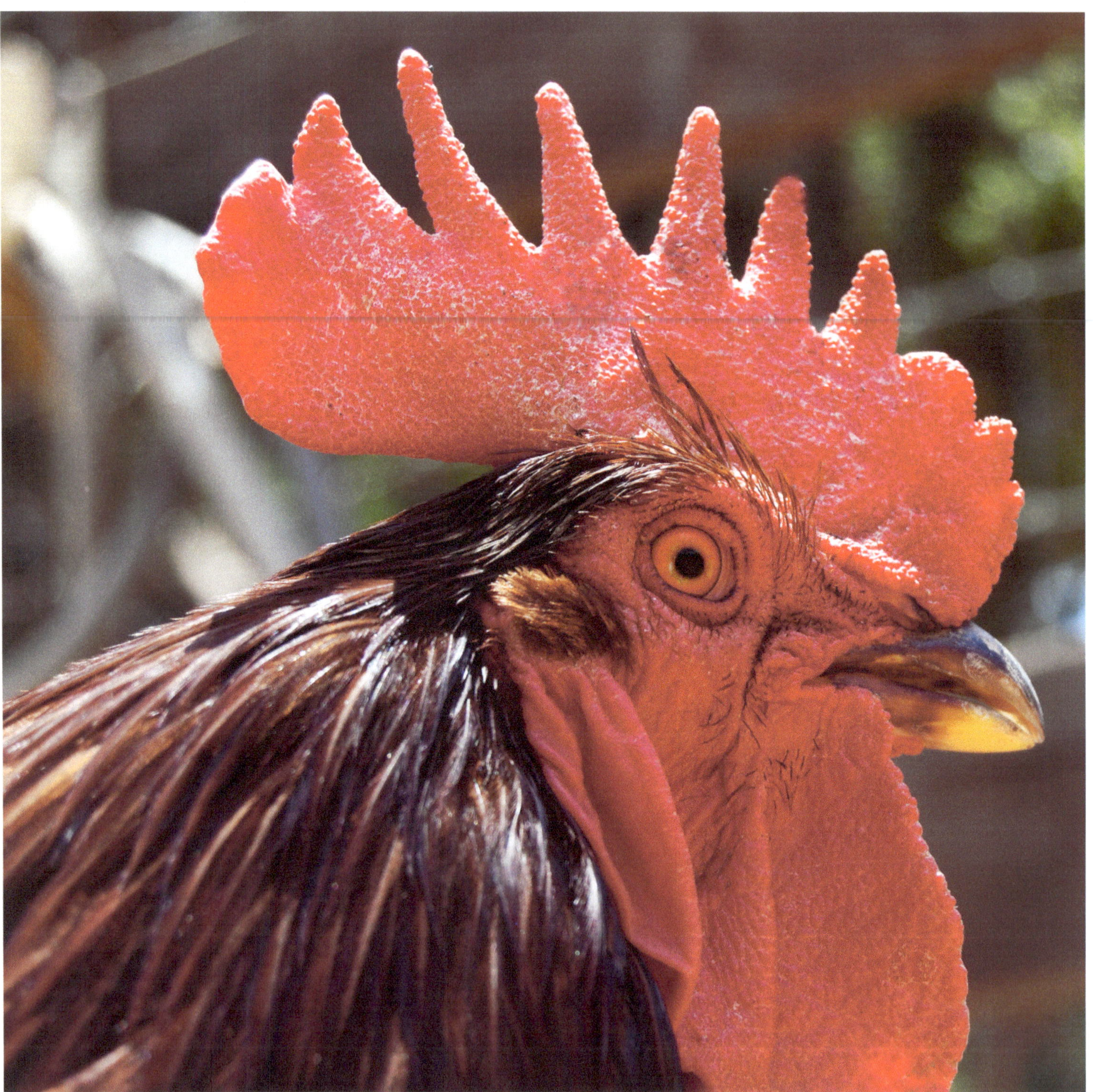

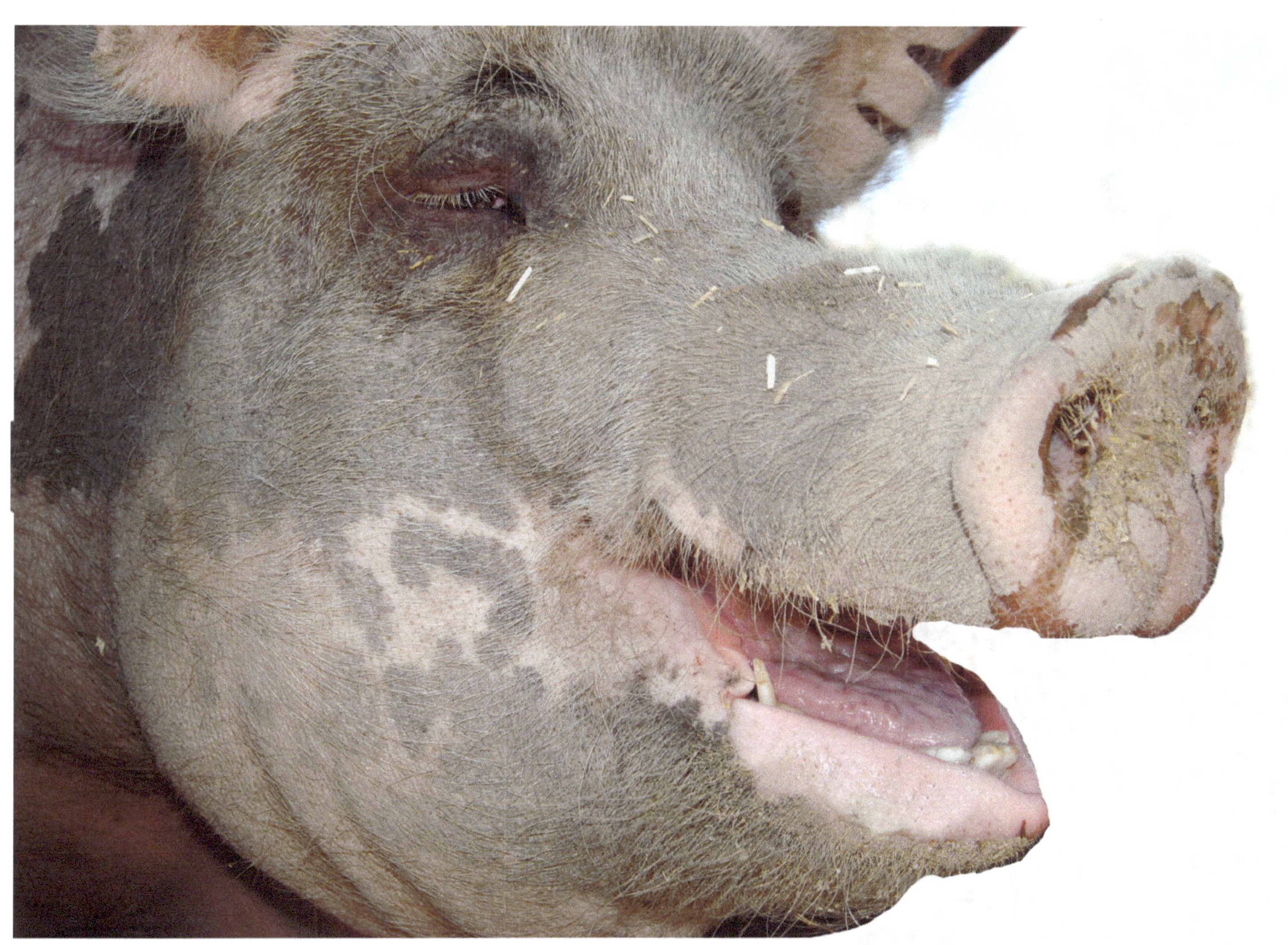

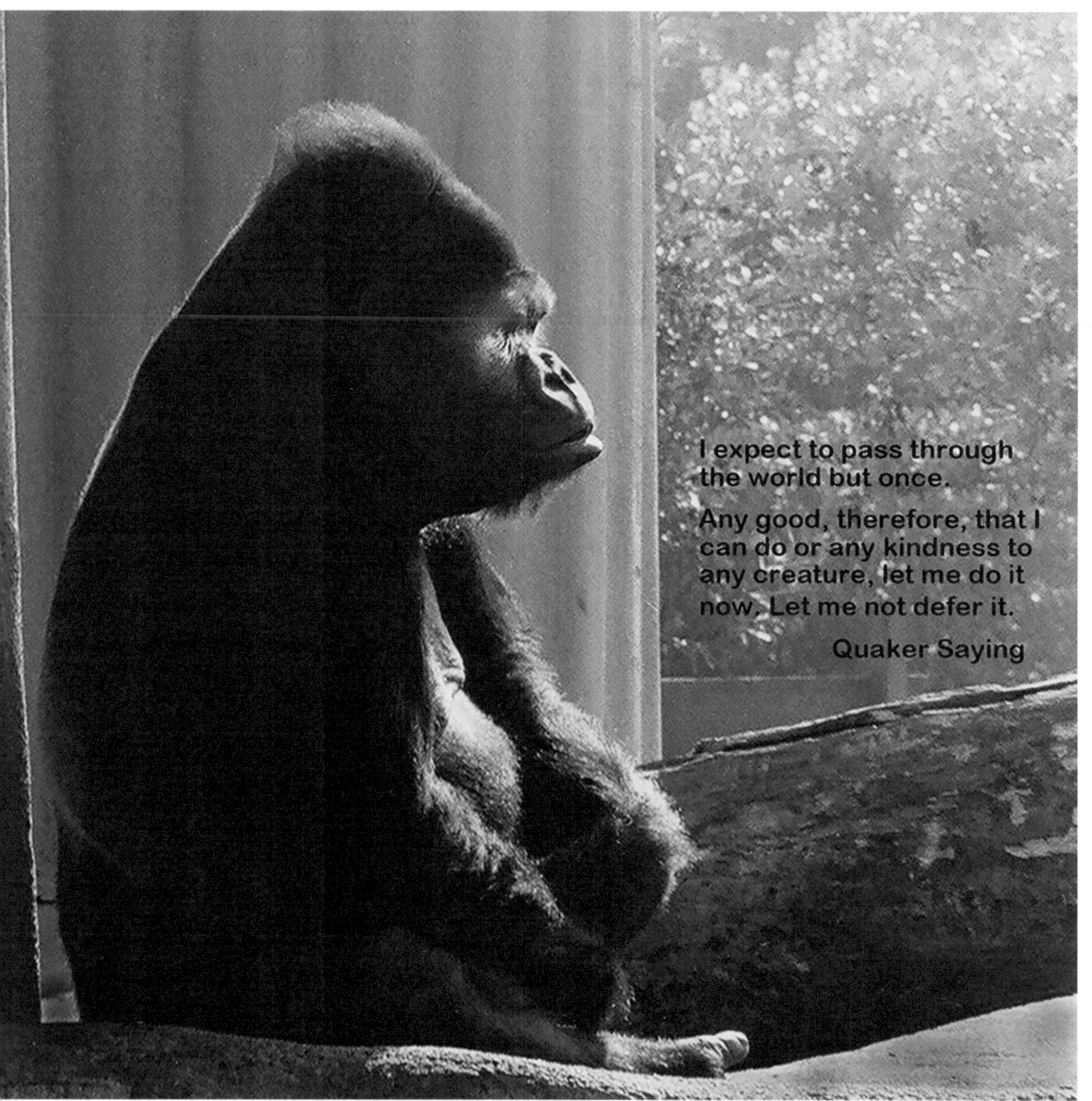
I expect to pass through
the world but once.

Any good, therefore, that I
can do or any kindness to
any creature, let me do it
now. Let me not defer it.

Quaker Saying

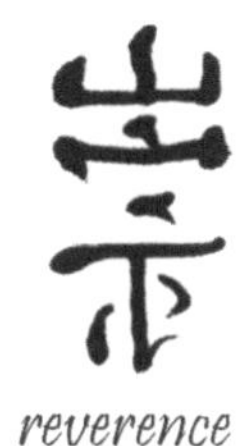

All beings are our companions on this planet. Extend your compassion to all. Love everyone and everything equally.

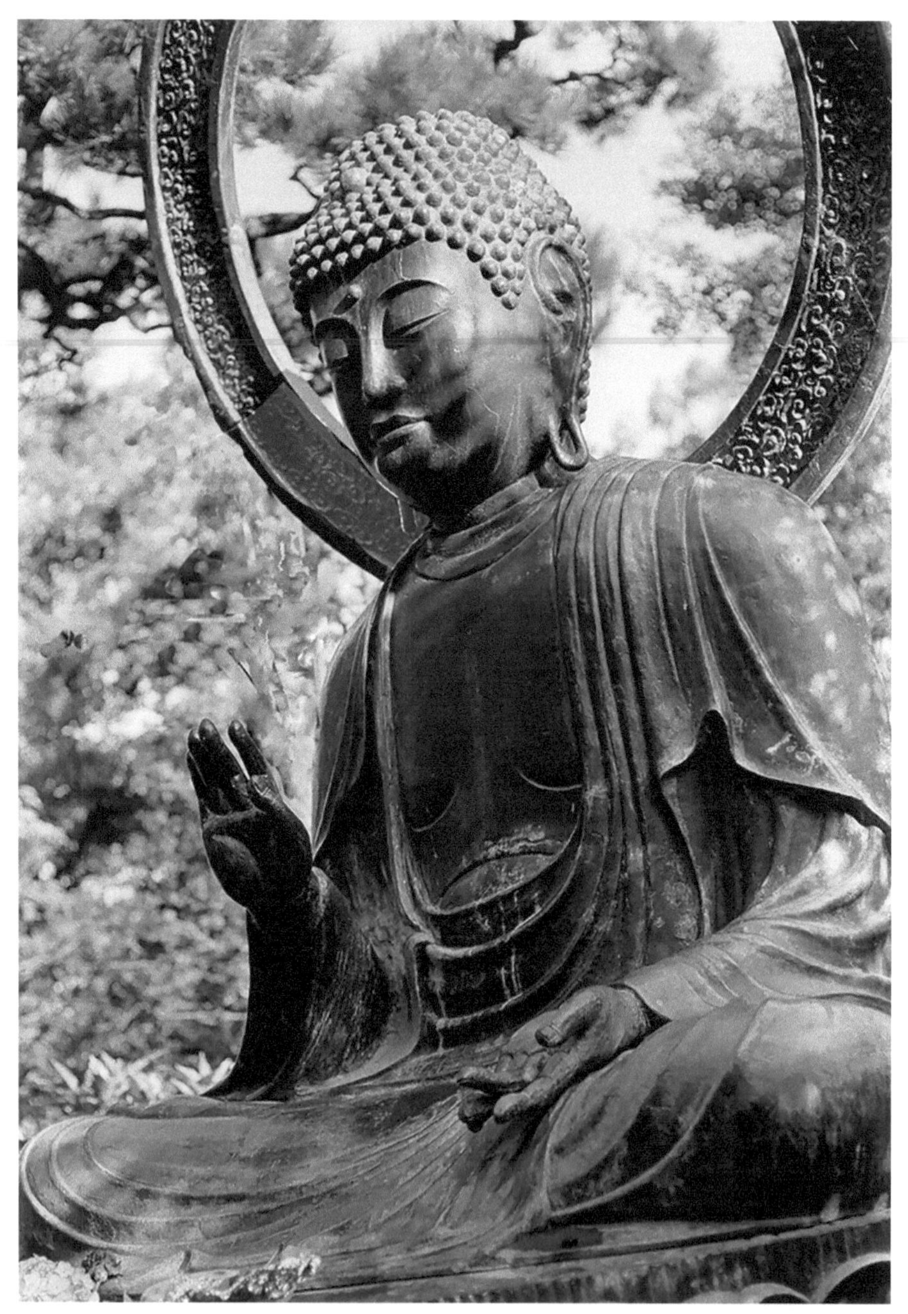

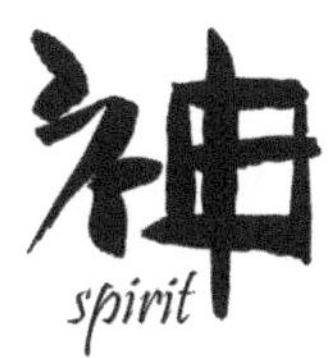

sitting in the heart of the Buddha
breathing deeply
filled with compassion
for all things

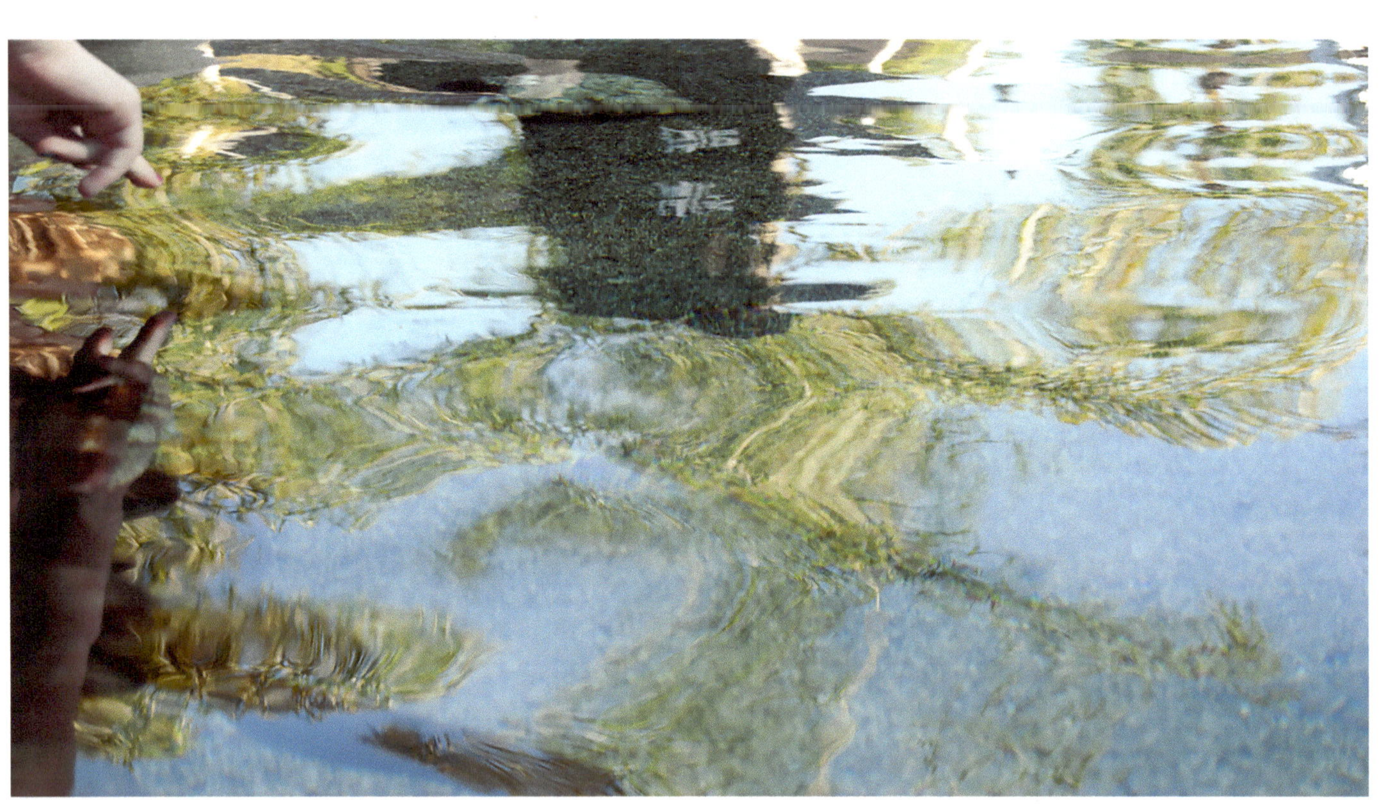

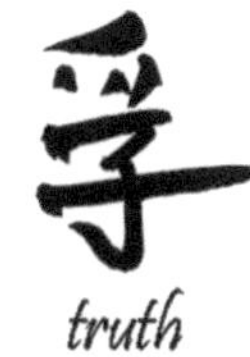

truth

Male:	Your hair was bright in the sunshine.
Female:	I don't like the sun. My skin is too pale. I live in the shade of too tall trees.
Male:	We fed the ducks. They crowded the banks and stole the food from our hands. It's best when they wait.
Female:	I remember the water drops on their backs. Silver on black. Nothing got through.
Male:	The bread soaked and sank. I said, "Next time we should bring lettuce."
Female:	My hand was in the water. I wanted to hold the wetness. It ran through me, through my hands, I mean.
Together:	I looked over. You were there by the water I took your hand...

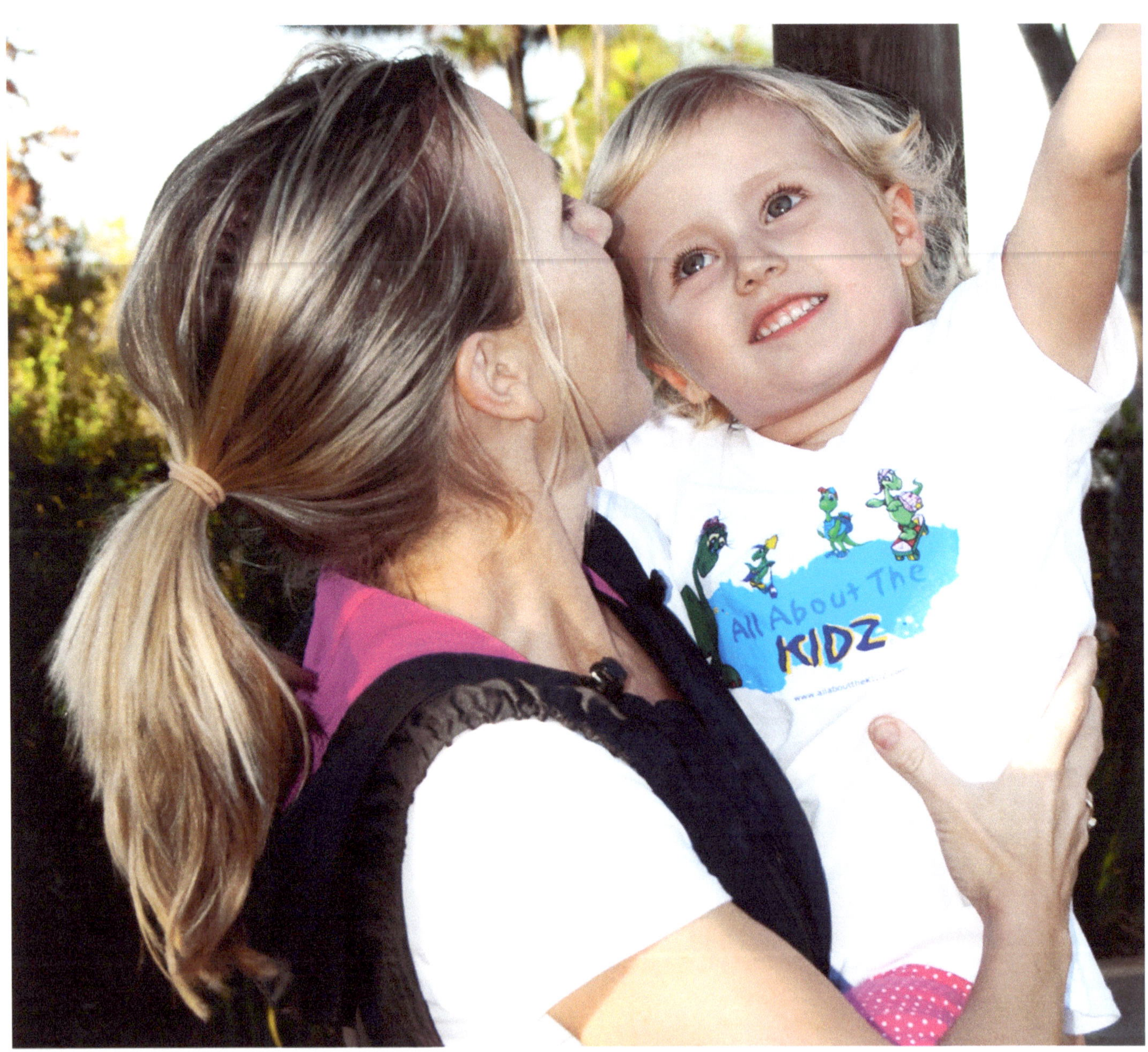

All About The
KIDZ
www.allaboutthek...

אַהֲבָה
love

As God's chosen people,
holy and dearly loved,
clothe yourself with
compassion, kindness
humility, gentleness
and patience.

Colossians 3-12

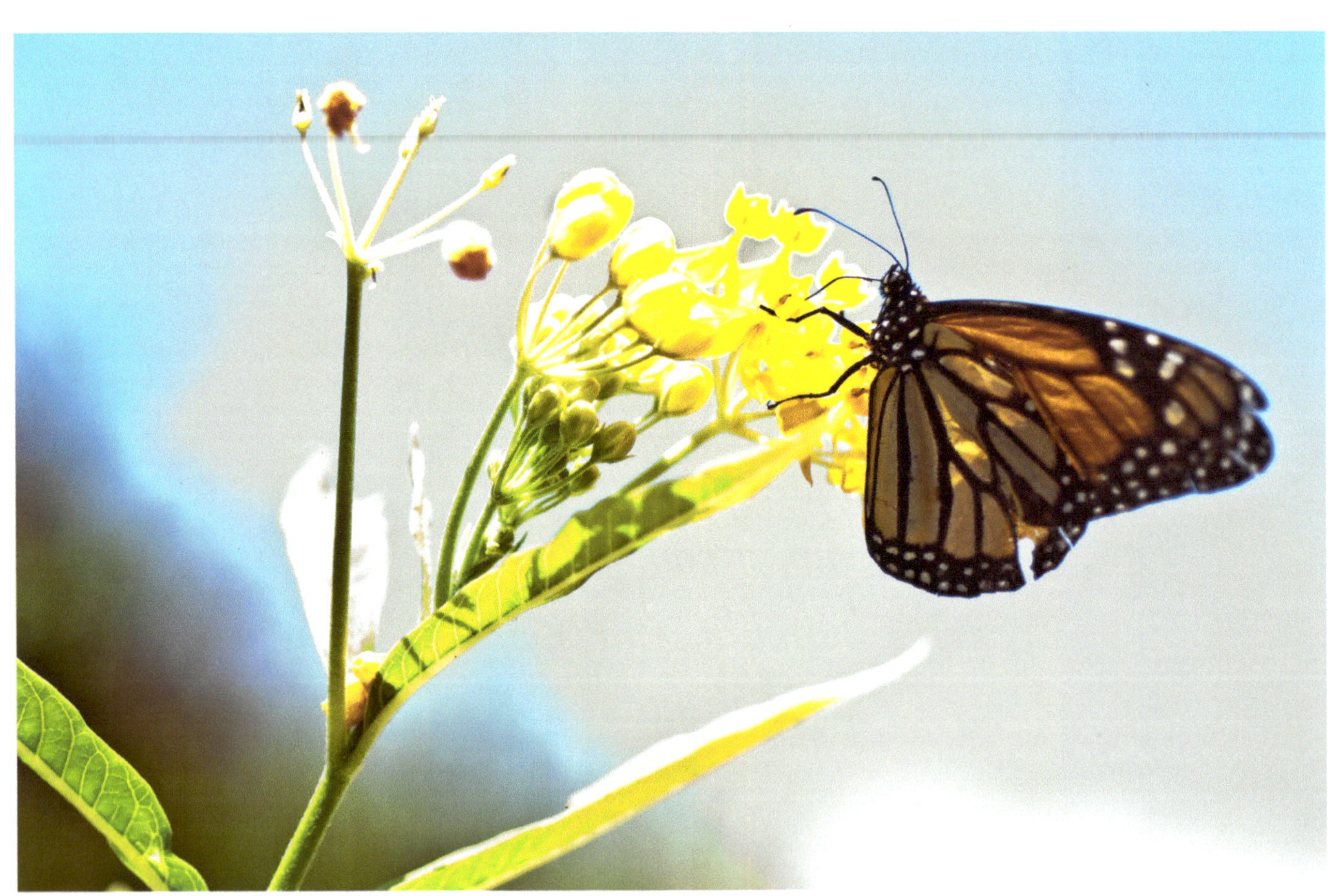

平 *peace*

there will be peace in this world
when everyone stops a moment
a watches the butterflies

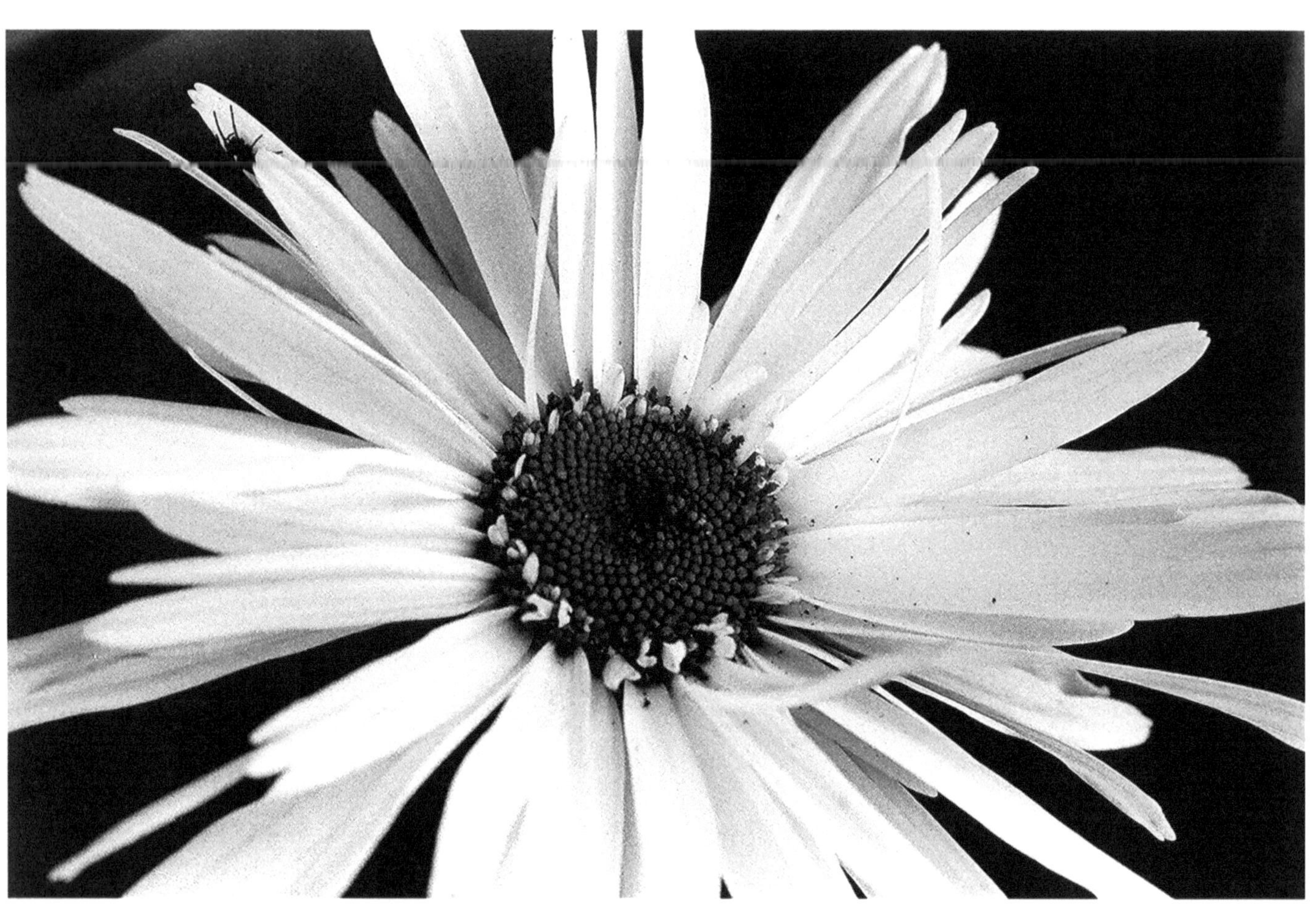

清

clarity

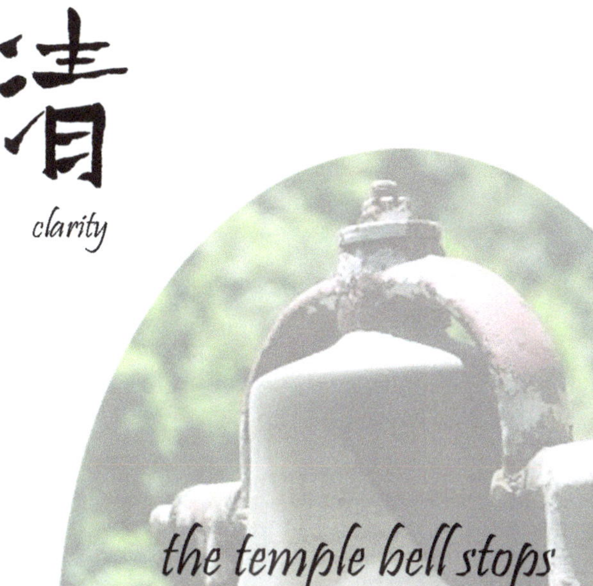

the temple bell stops
but the sound keeps coming
out of the flowers

Basho

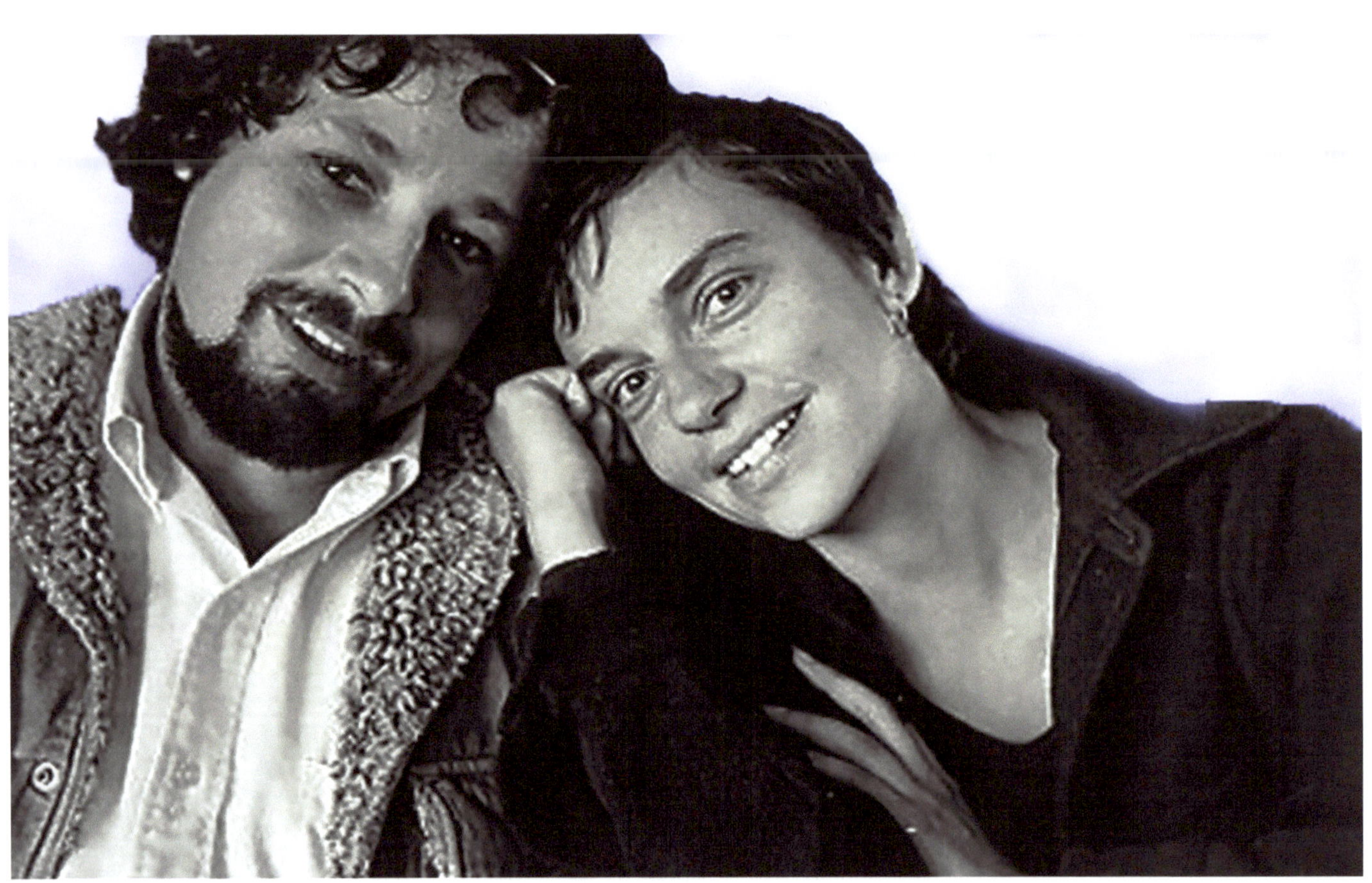

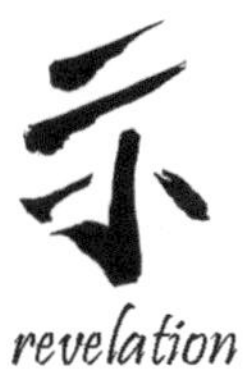 *revelation*

Love transforms you.
It's not something you think about.
It's something in which you live.

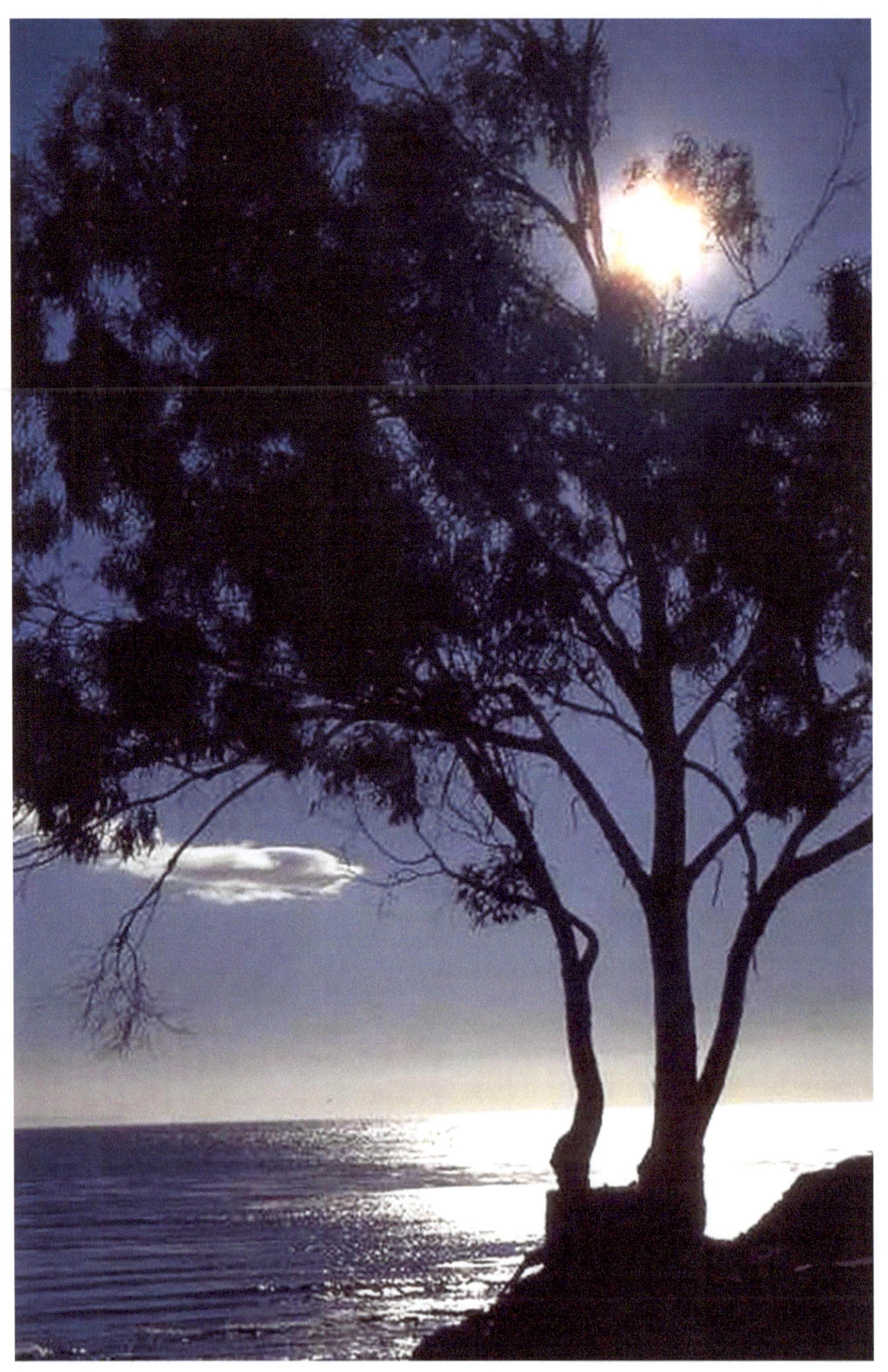

生活
life

From every human being there shines a light that reaches straight to heaven. When two souls that are destined to be together find each other, the streams of light flow together and a single, brighter light goes forth from that united being.

The Baal Shem Tov

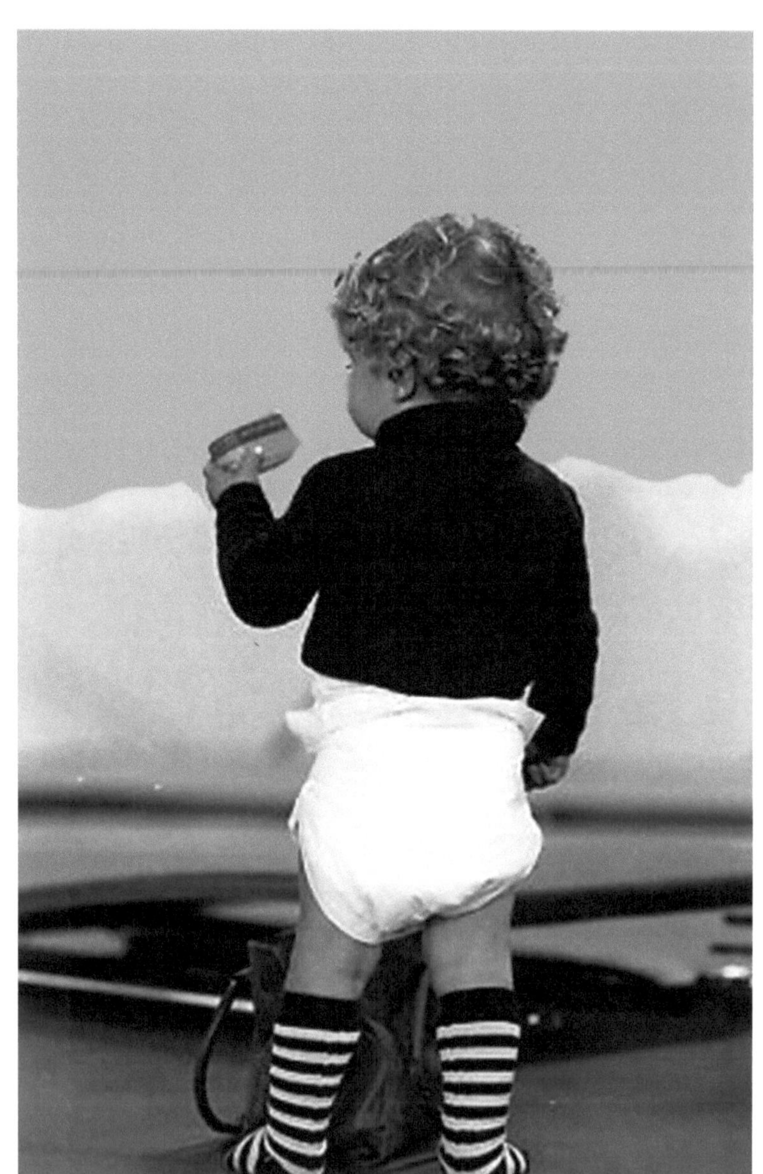

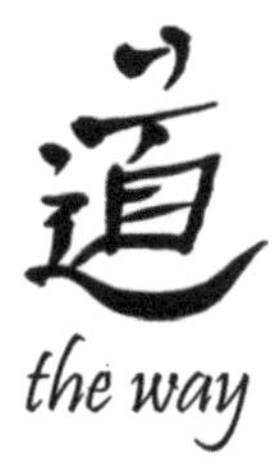

the way

How wonderful!

All things perfect
exactly as they are.

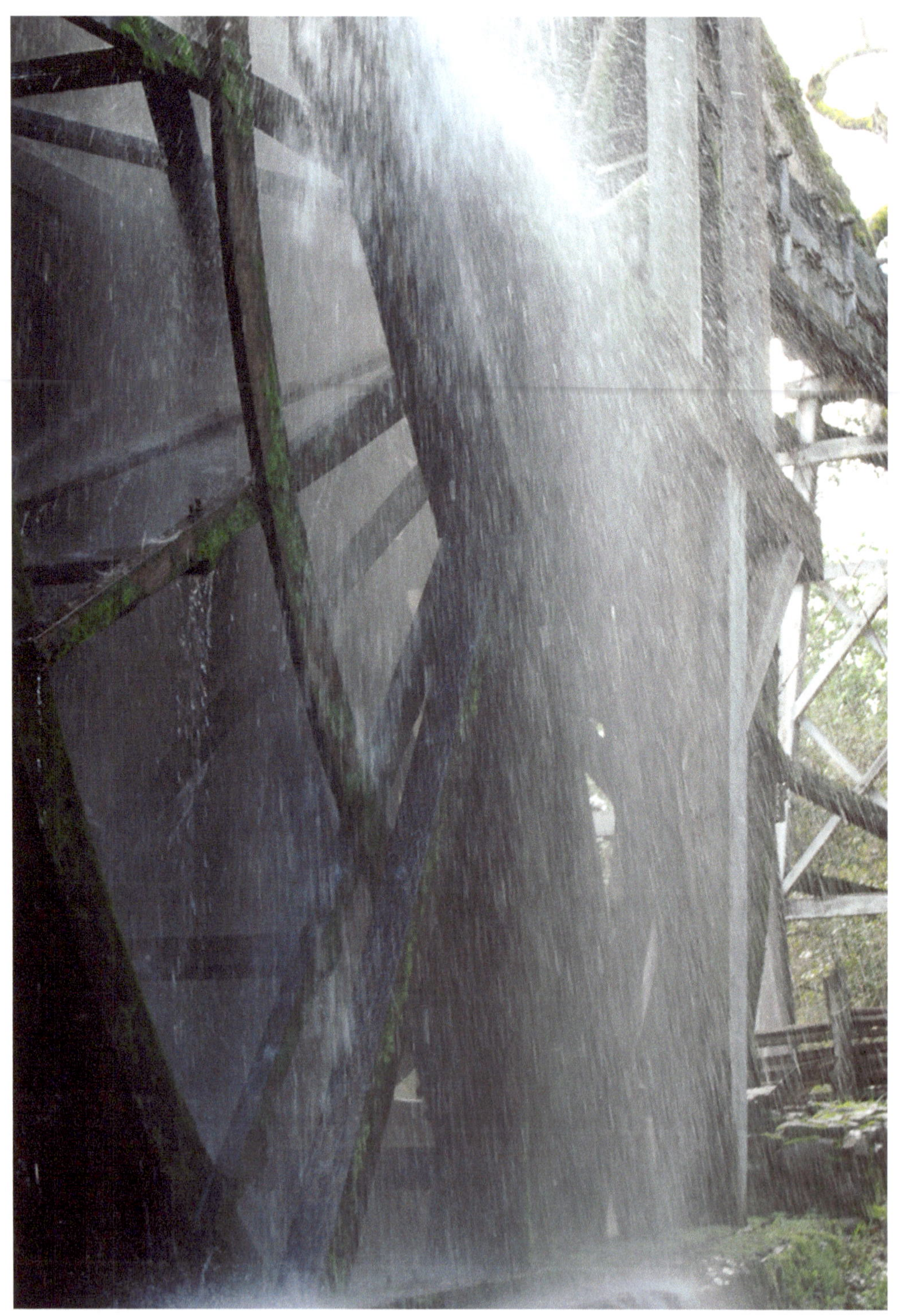

Zen

With wisdom and truth
discipline and self-control
the wise become like islands
that no flood can overwhelm

Buddha
from the Dharmapada

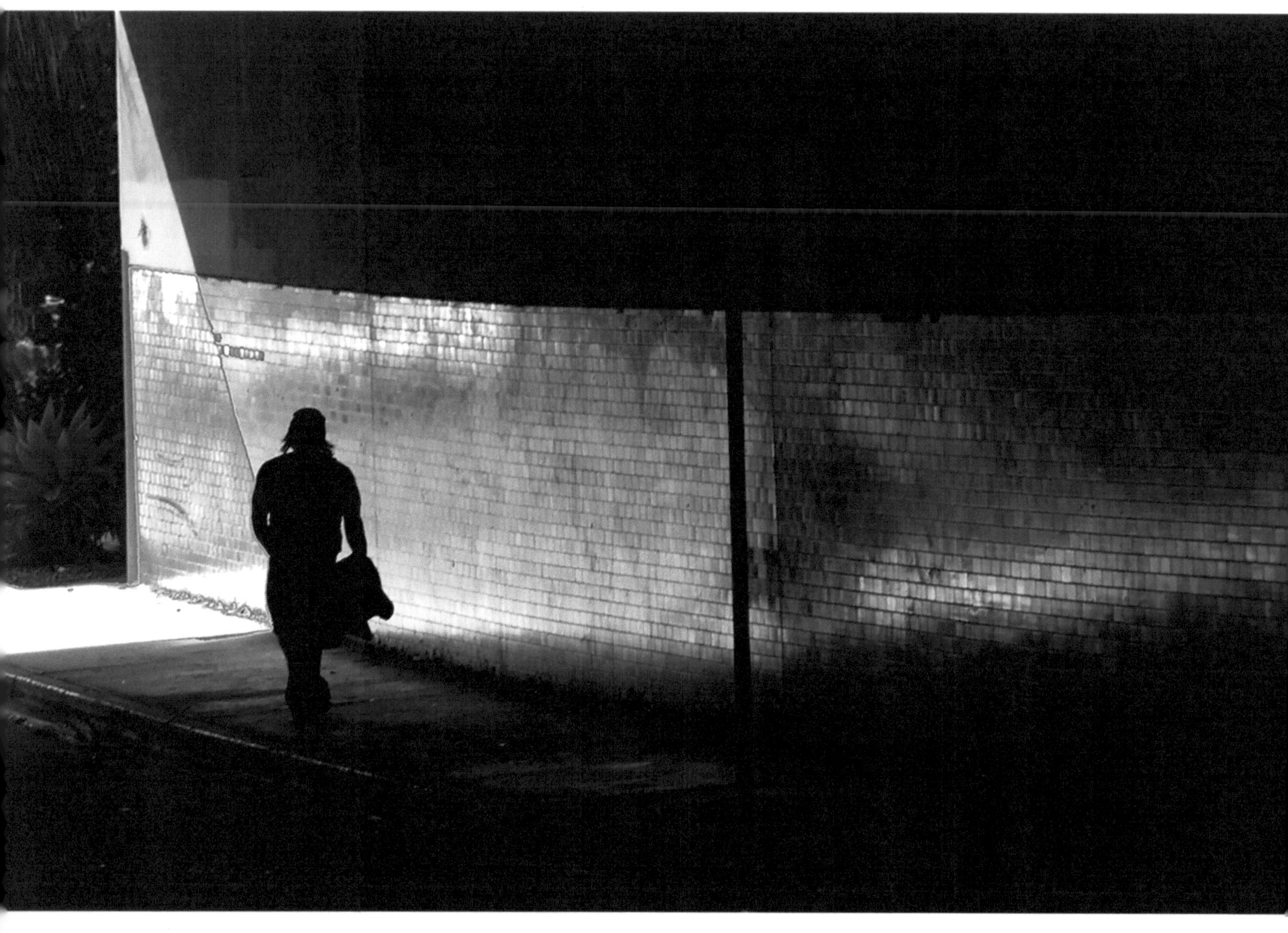

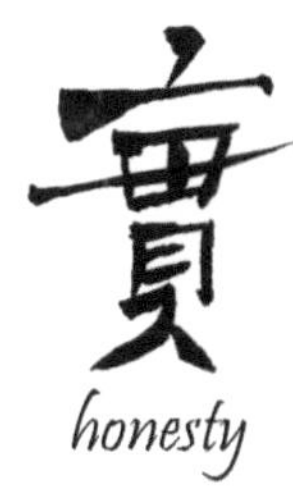

honesty

if you find no master

travel alone

Zen saying

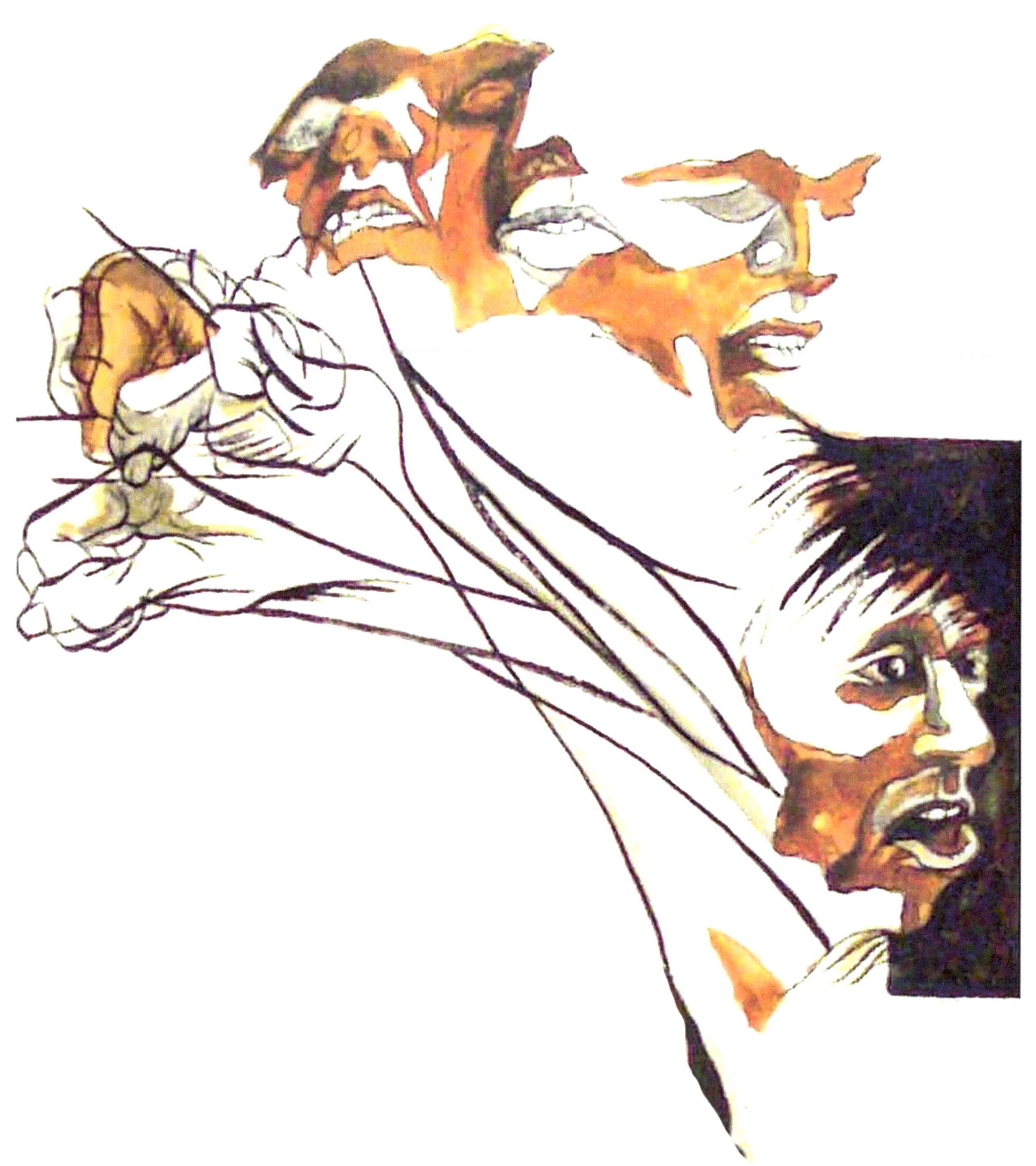

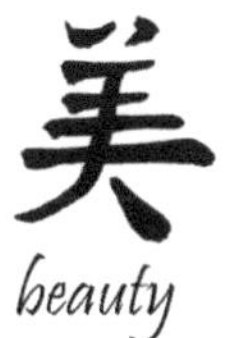
beauty

small doubt small enlightenment
big doubt big enlightenment

Buddha

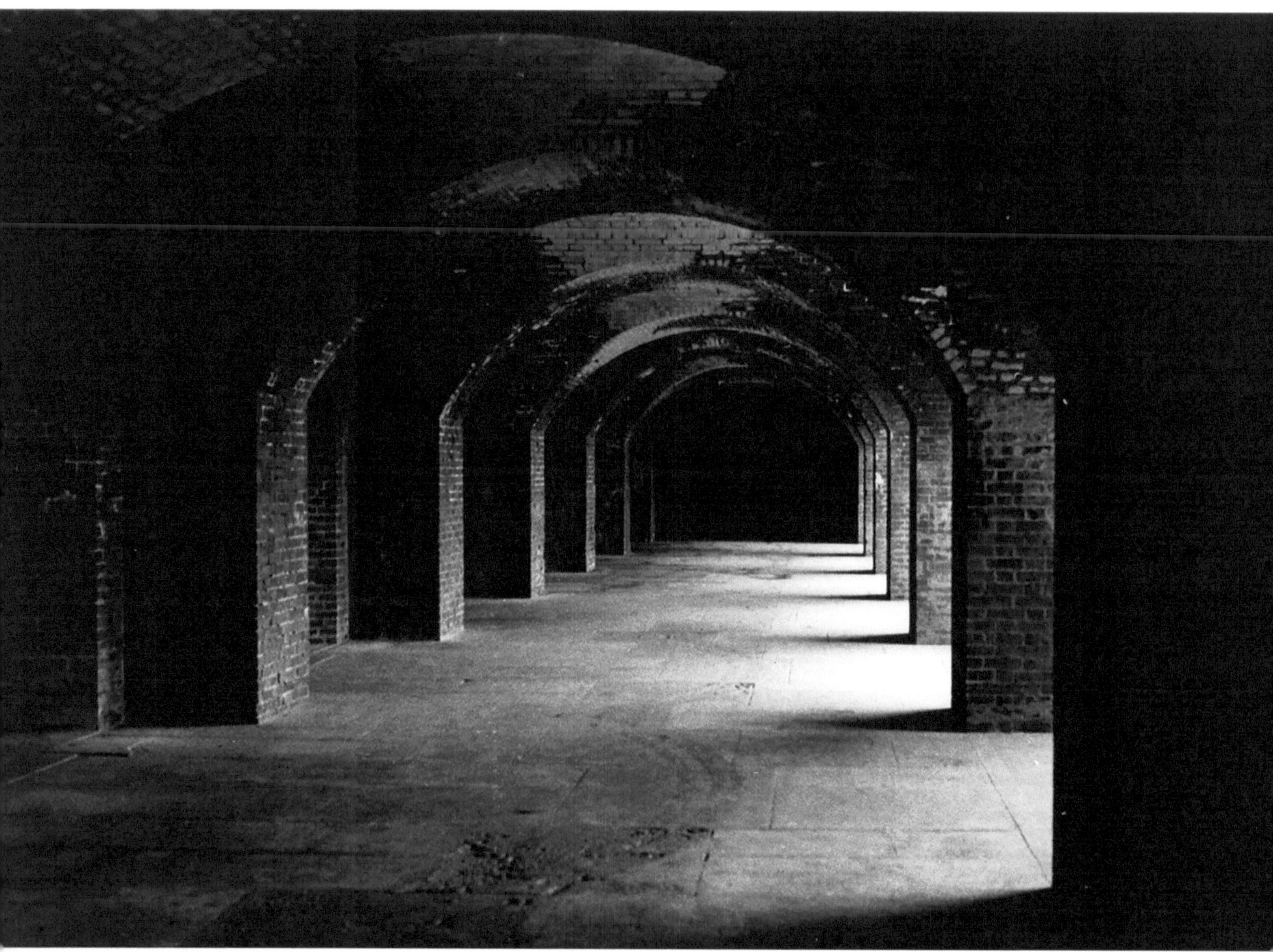

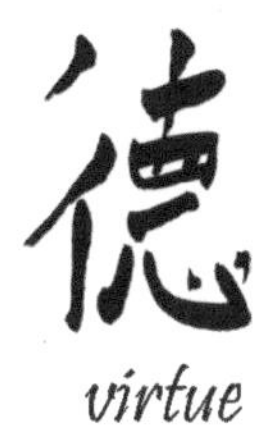

virtue

To study Buddah's way is to study the self

To study self is to transcend self

To transcend self is to be enlightened by all things

To be enlightened by all things is to remove the barrier between self and others

This is the path to compassion

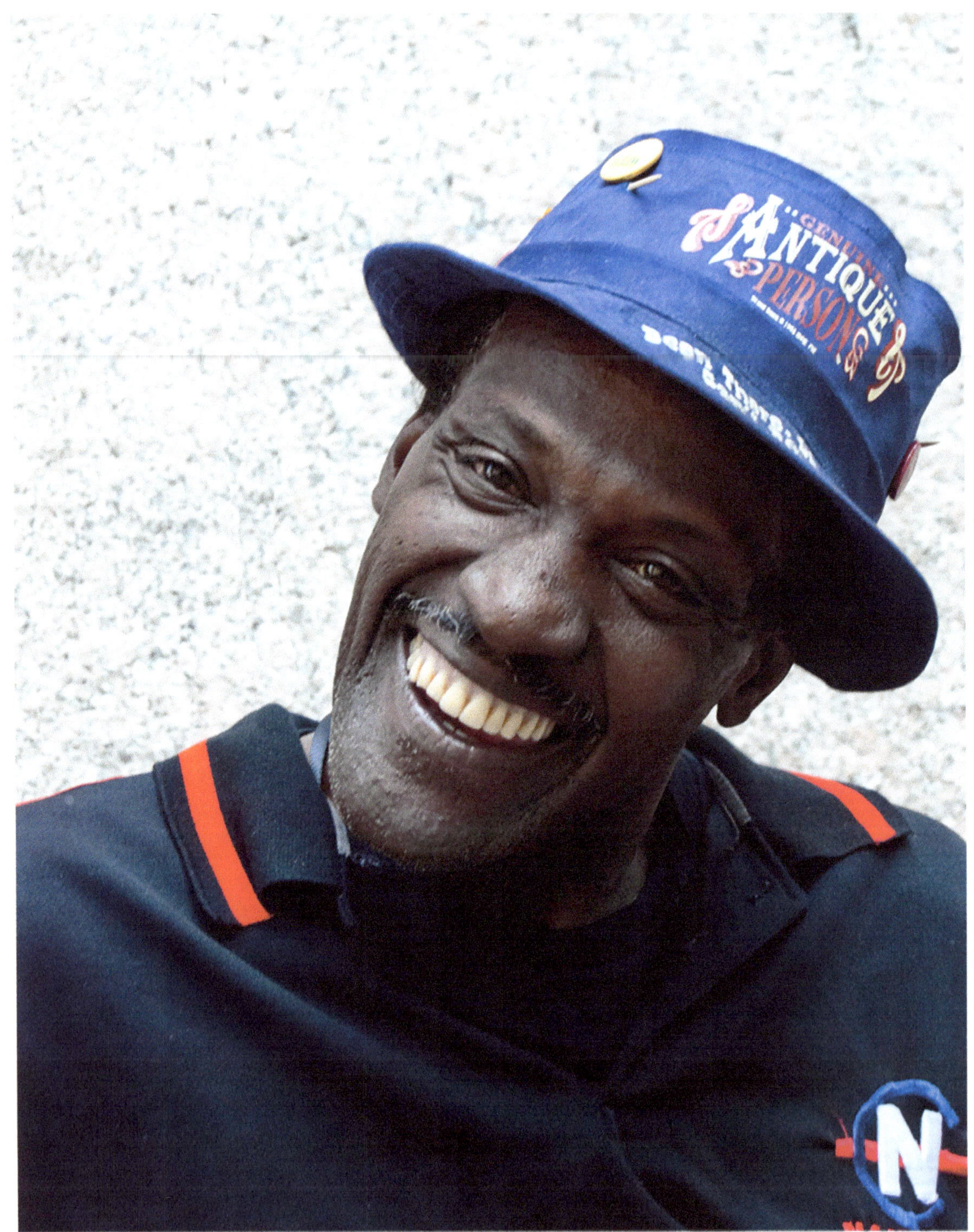
GENUINE
ANTIQUE
PERSON

生活

life

This moment is yours

Live it fully

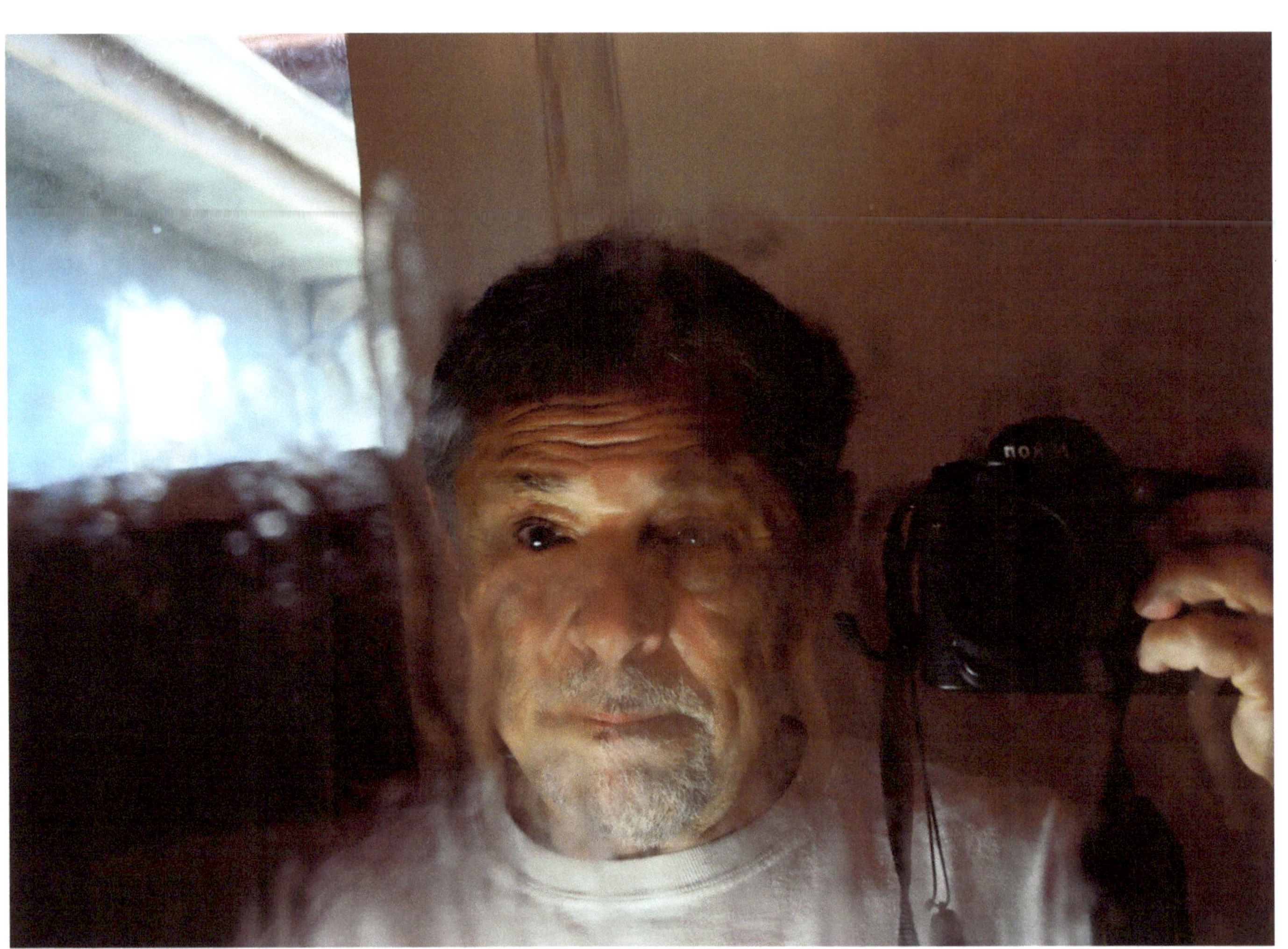

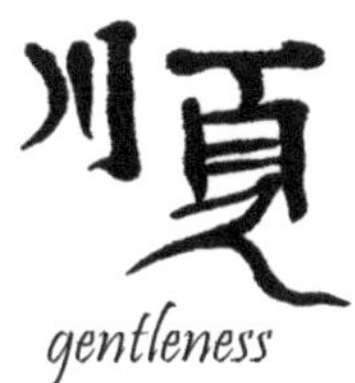

gentleness

We are of this world
not separate from it

Suspend reason

walk in magic

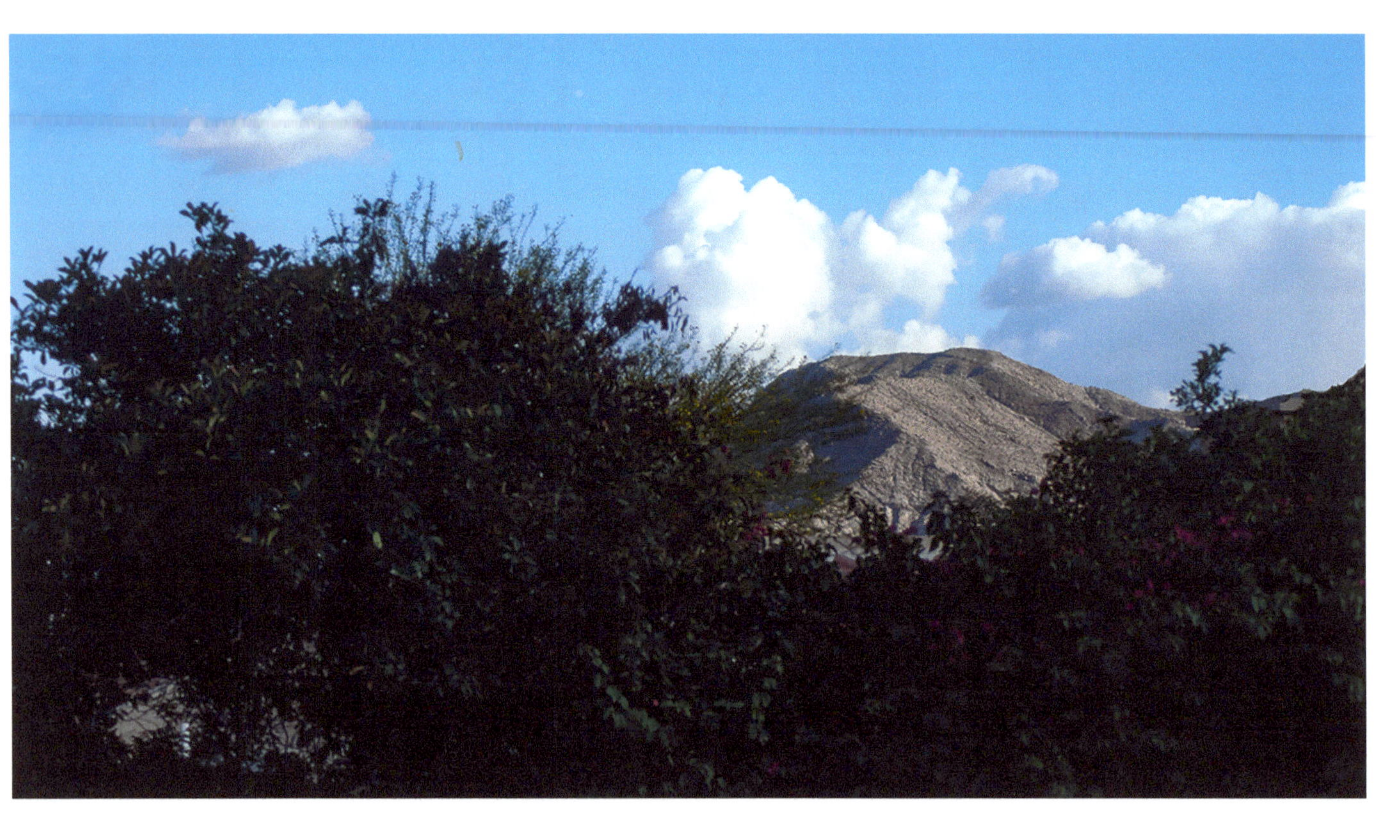

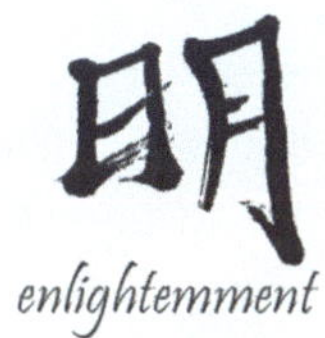

enlightemment

Hand in hand
climbing Mount Fuji
your steps are light

floating on compassion
as endless
as Buddha's smile

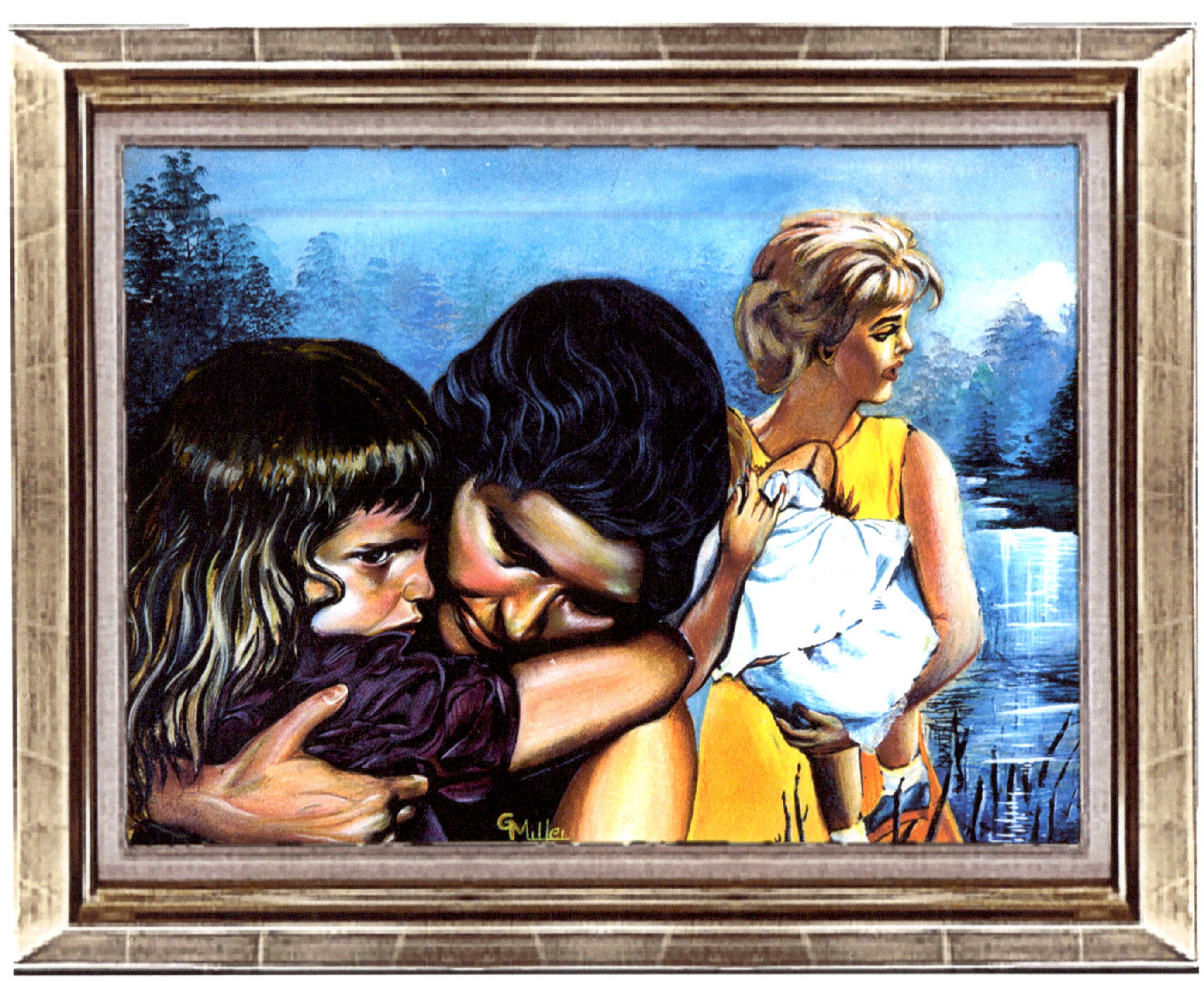

G Miller

关心
caring

The greatest disease ... is being
unwanted. unloved , and uncared
for. We can cure physical disease
with medicine. but the only cure
for despair, lonliness and hopelessness
is love.

Mother Teresa

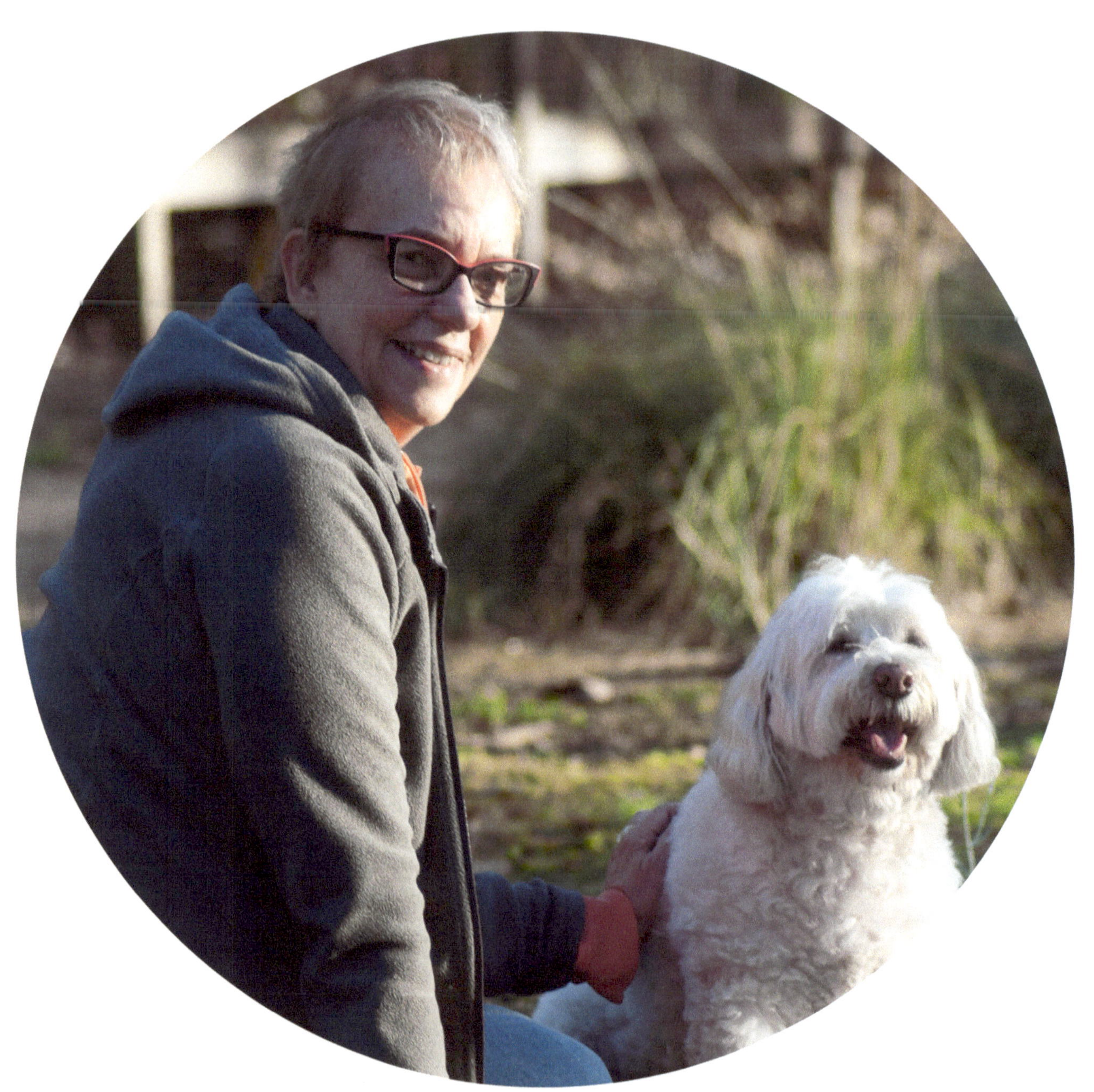

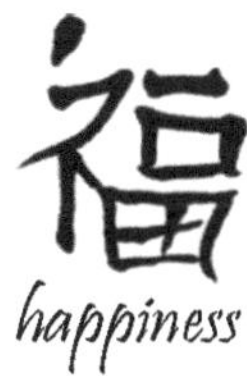

happiness

In true love you obtain freedom.

Thich Nhat Hahn

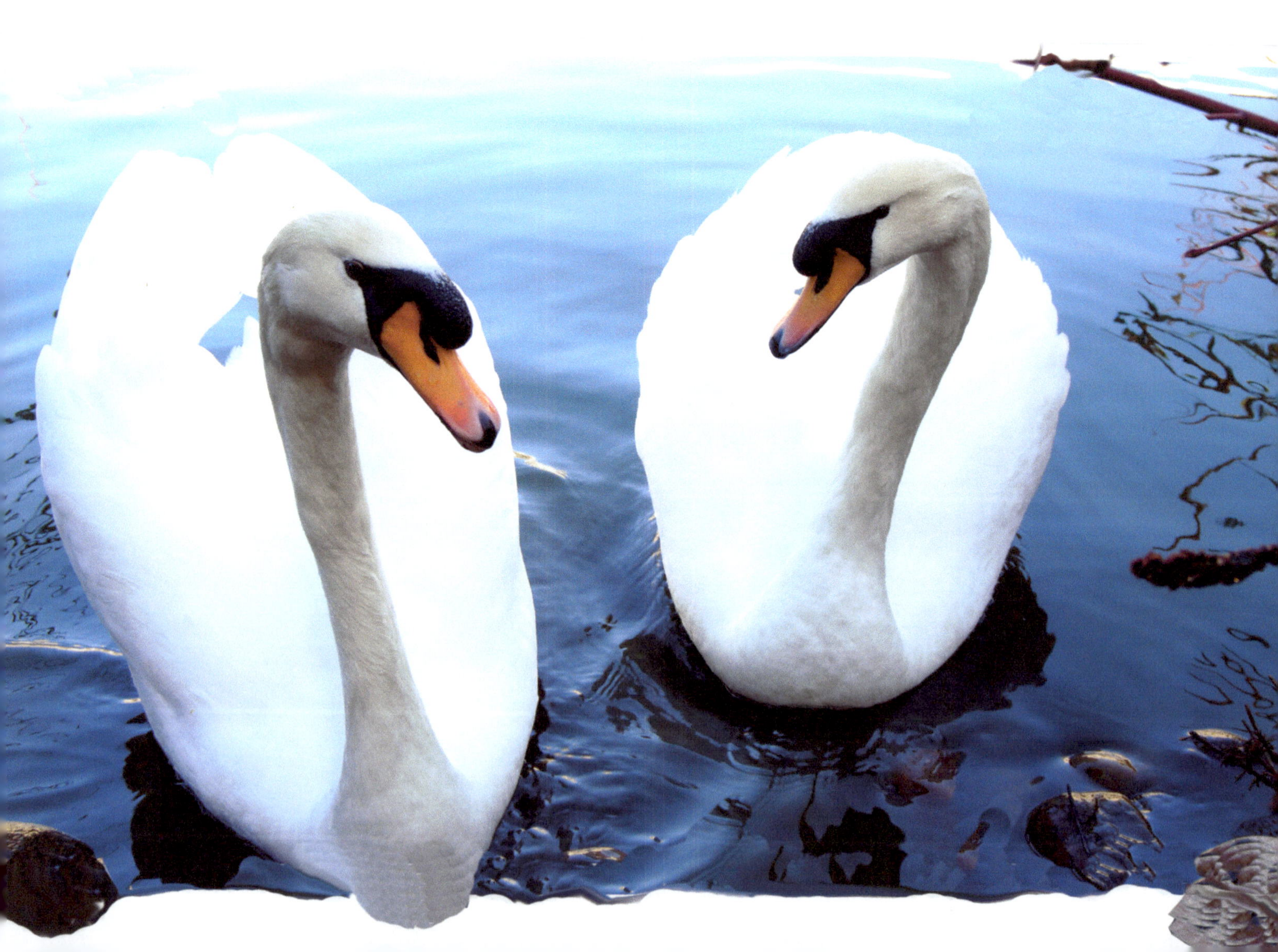

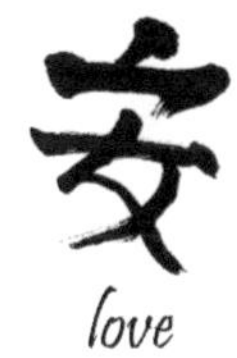

The highest state of love
is the unity of one soul
in two bodies

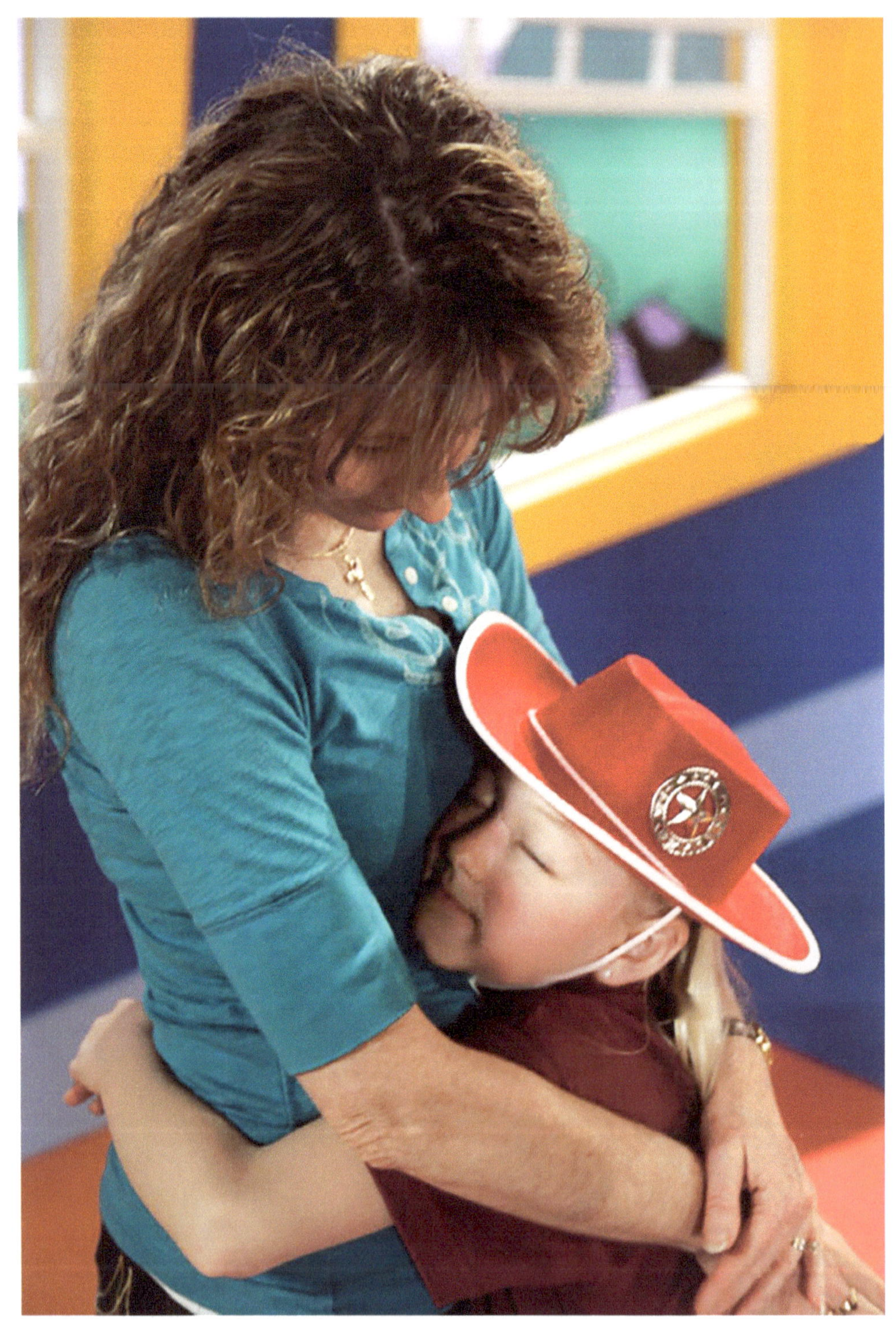

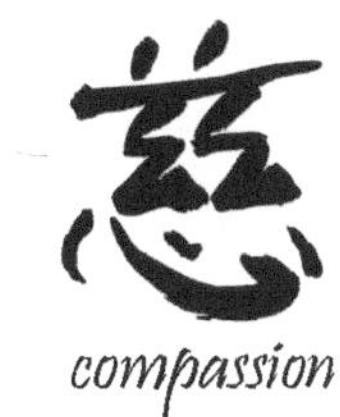

compassion

A hug should not just be something we do. A hug must be heartfelt, a connection between two beings that locks them, for that one moment, as two souls in one body.

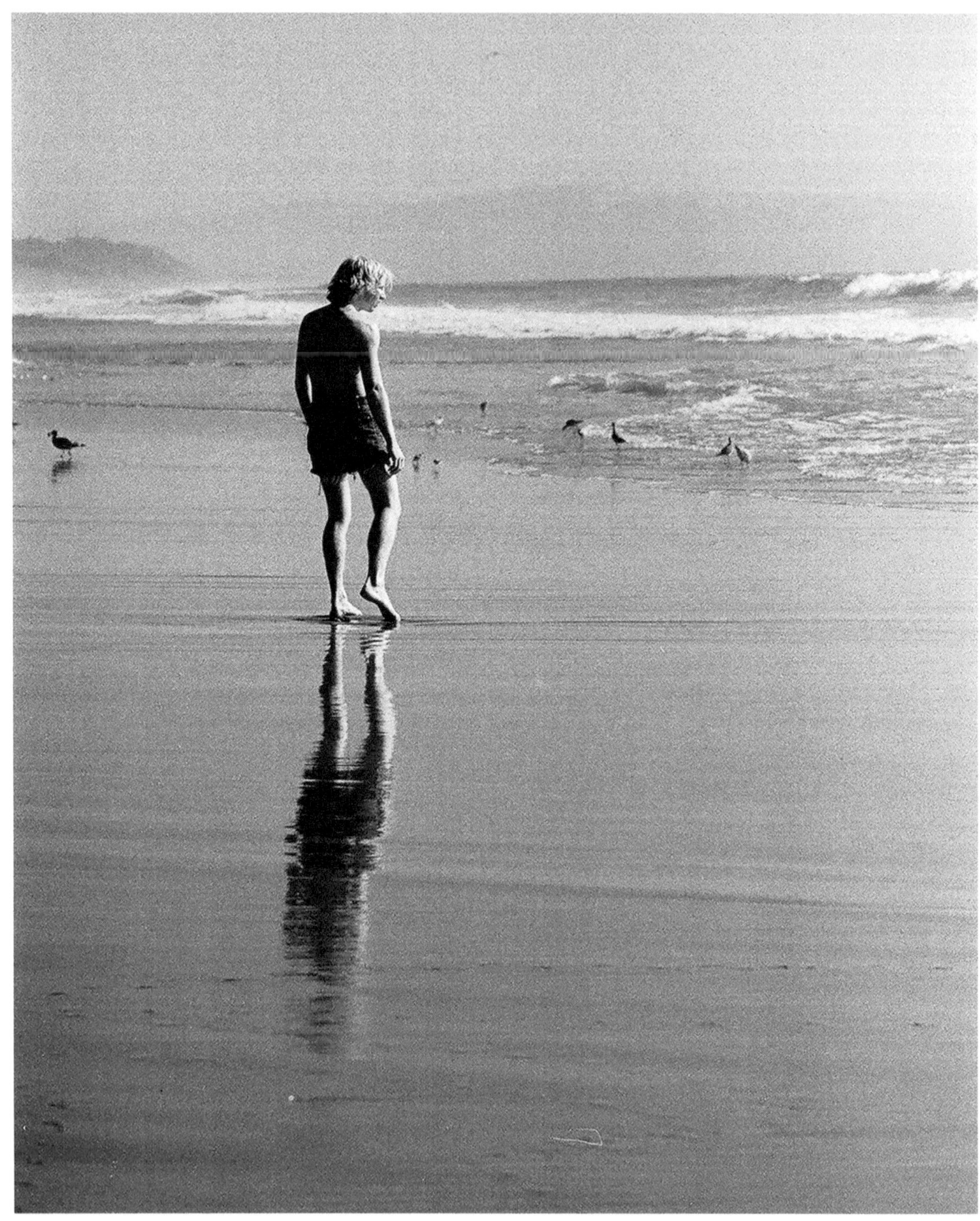

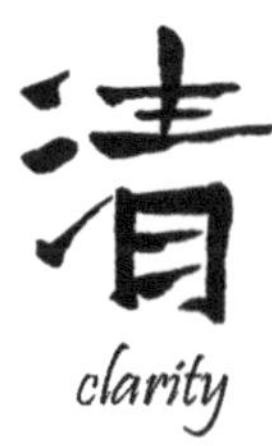

clarity

Dwelling in the present moment
I know this is the only moment.

Thich Nhat Hanh

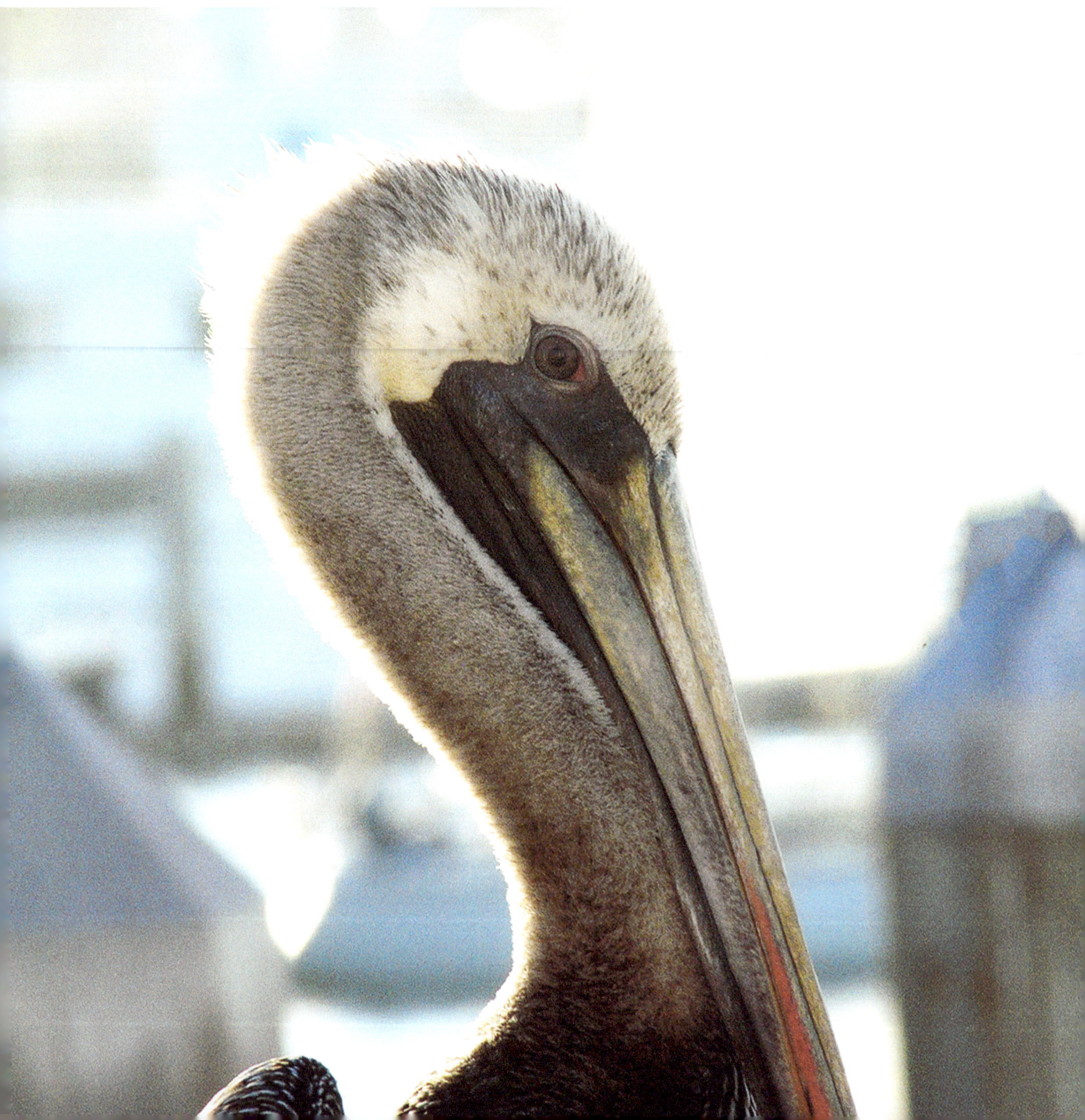

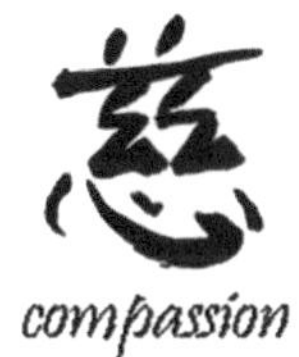

compassion

When one has compassion for all living beings, only then are they noble.

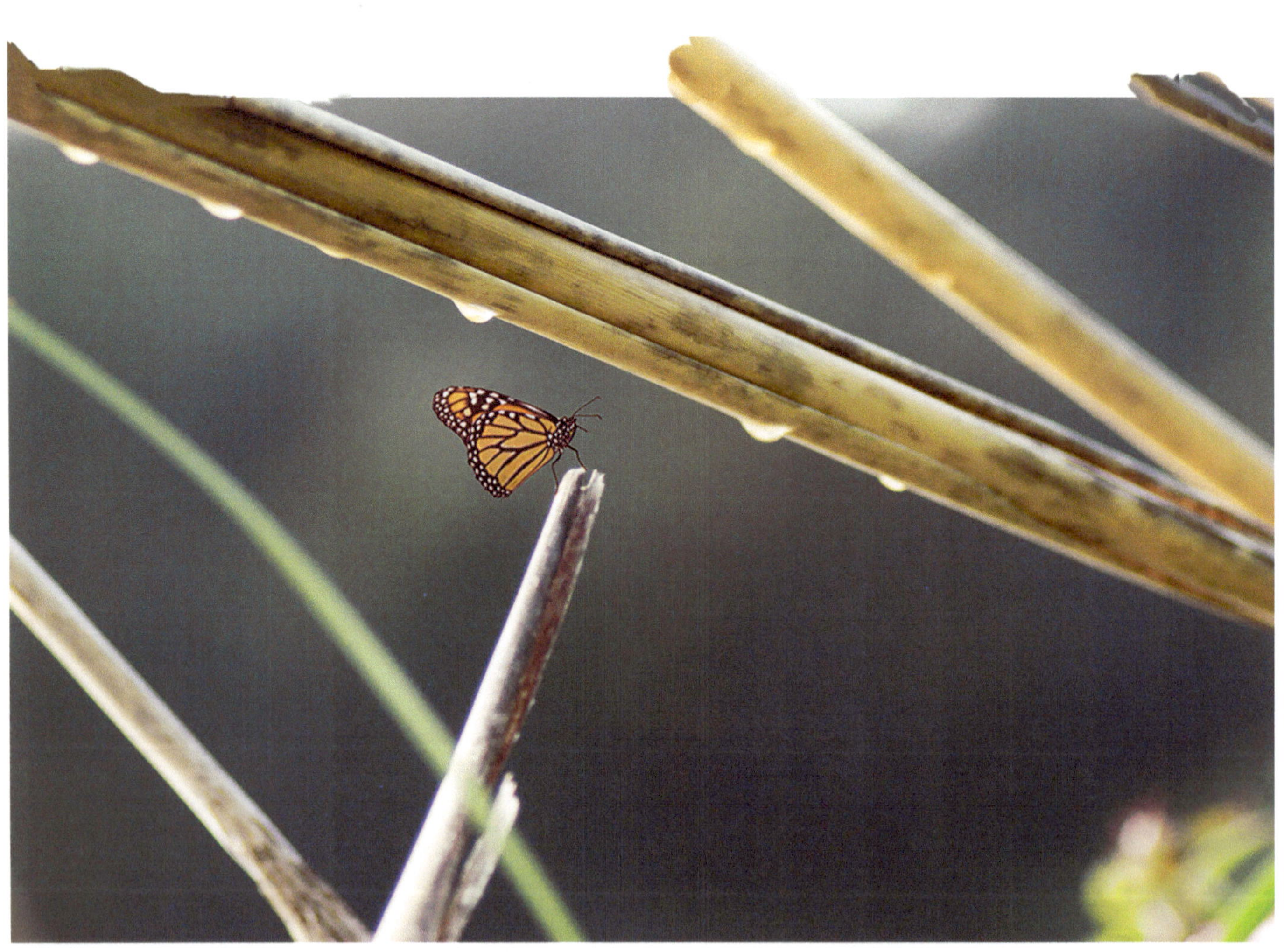

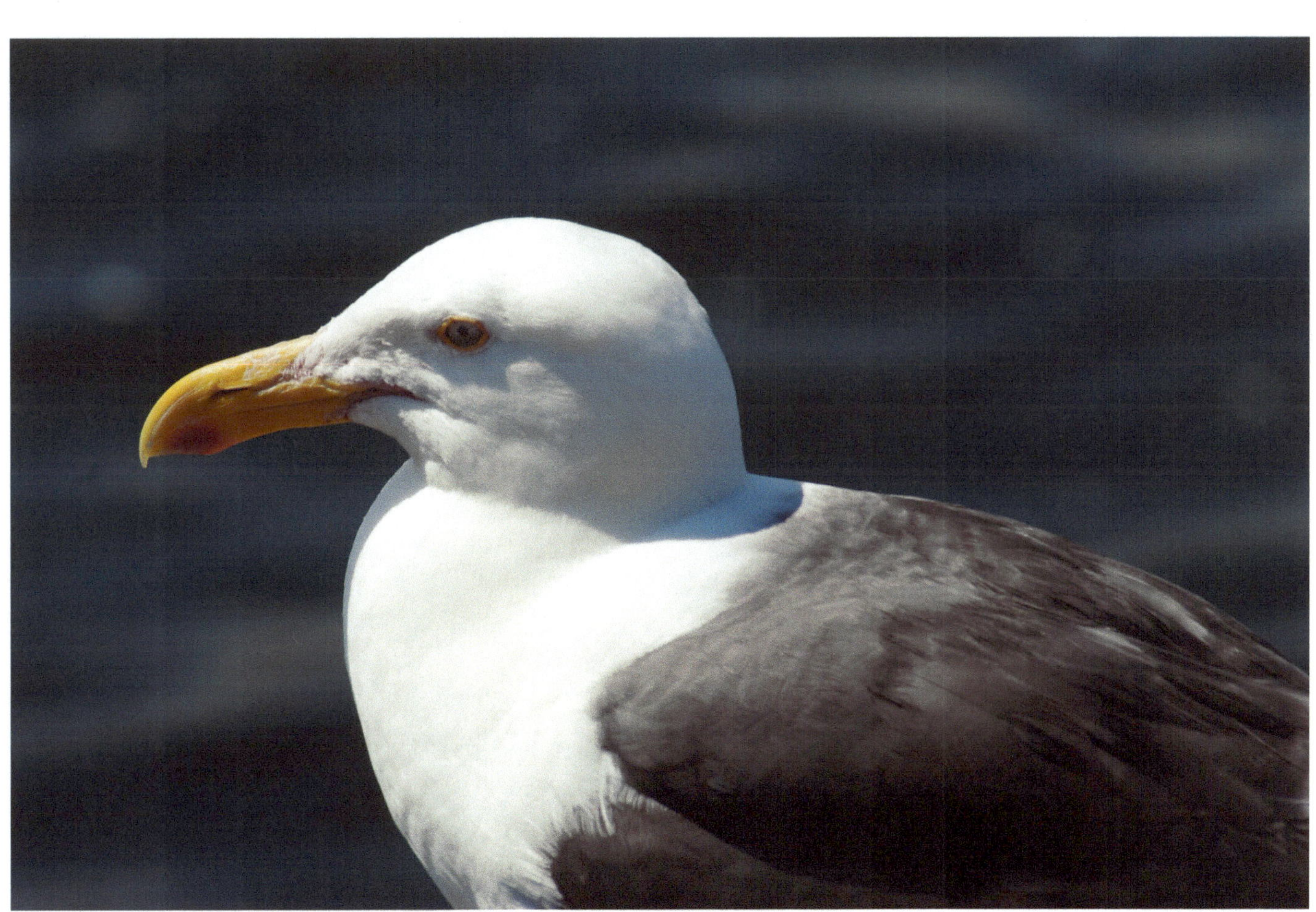

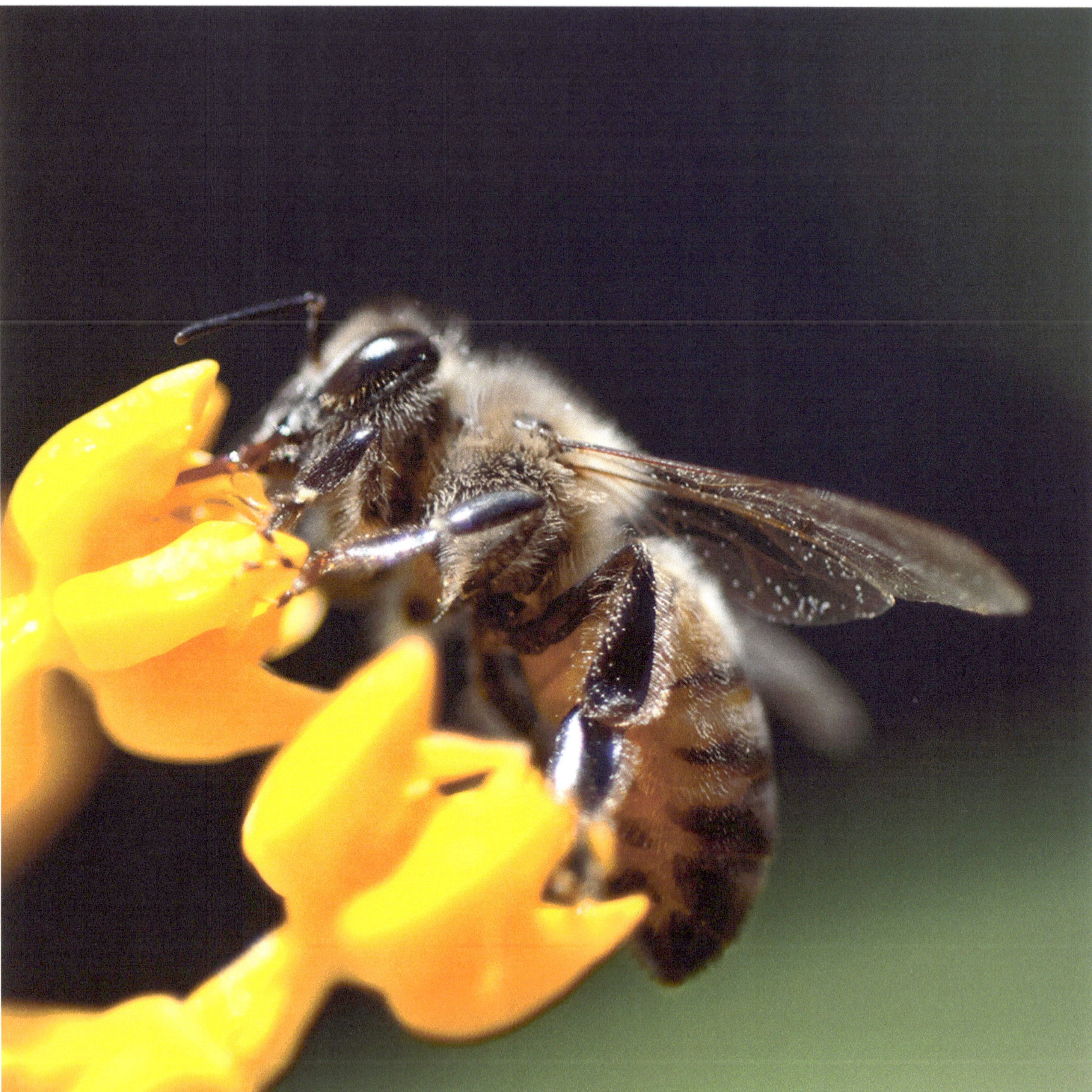

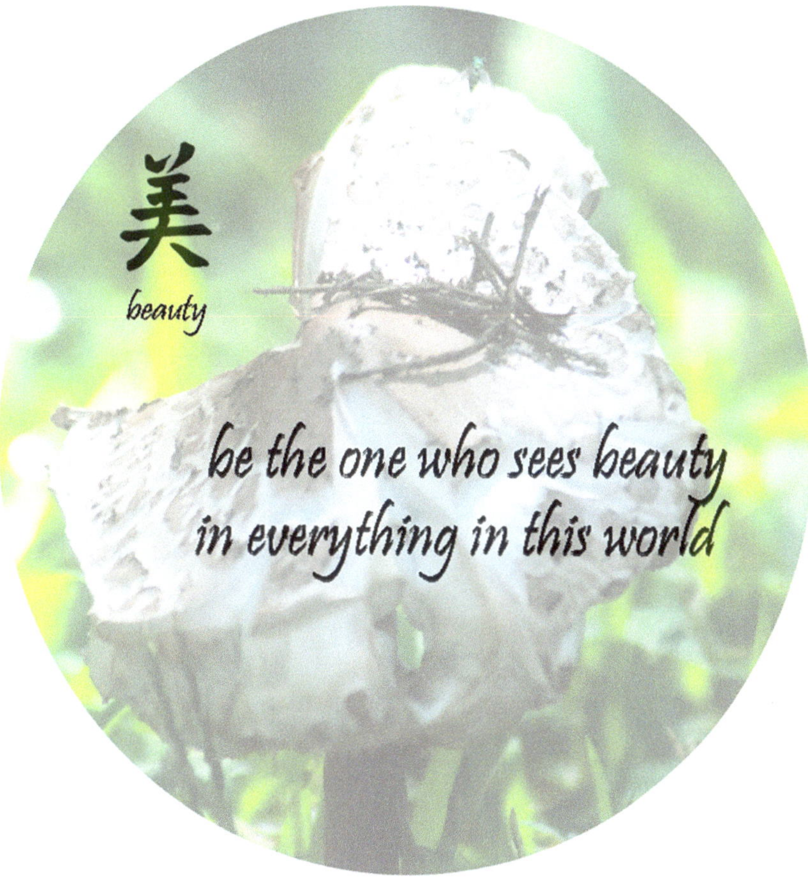
美
beauty
be the one who sees beauty
in everything in this world

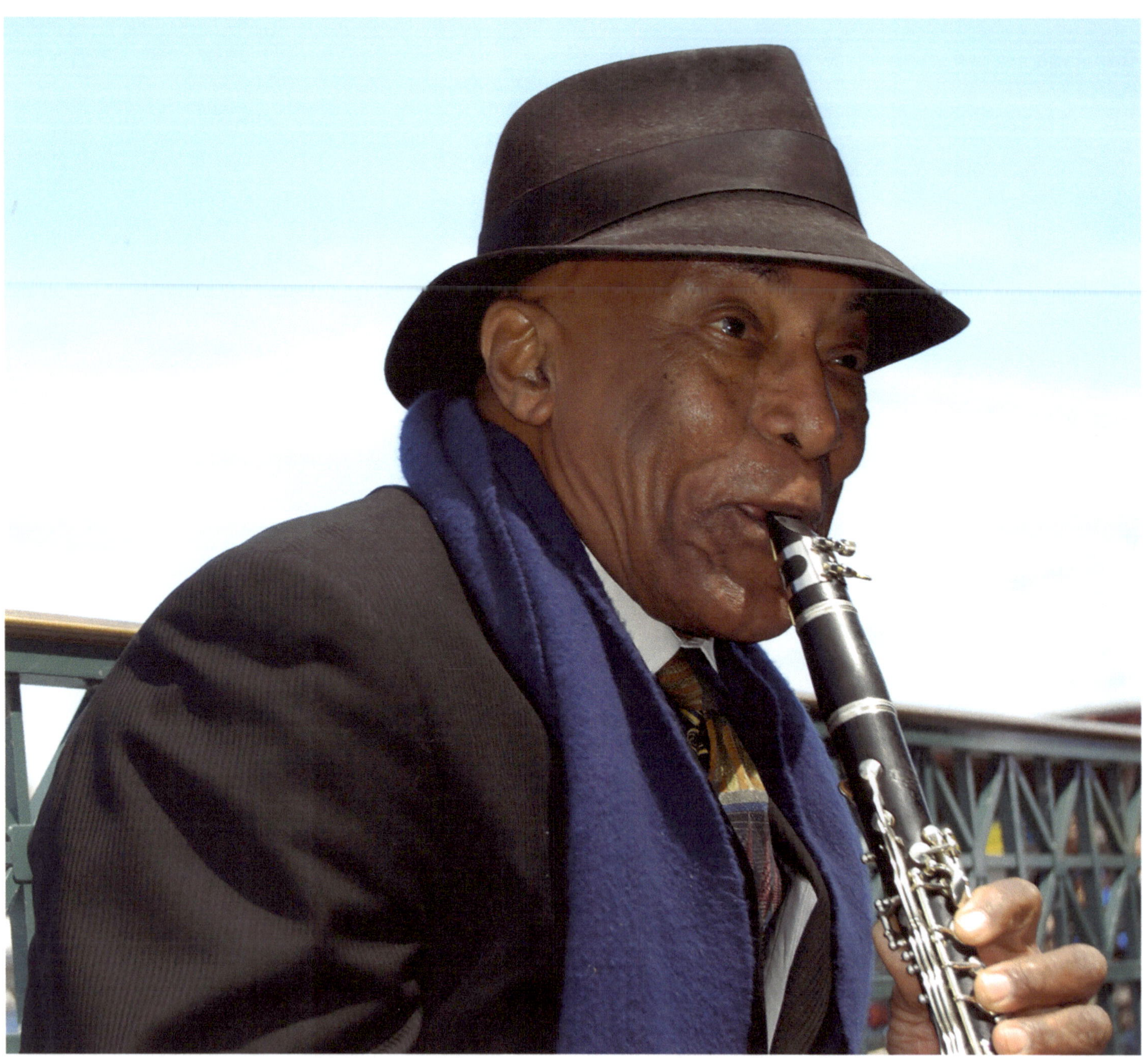

人 人
people

Compassion is the wish
to see others
free from suffering.

The Dalai Lama

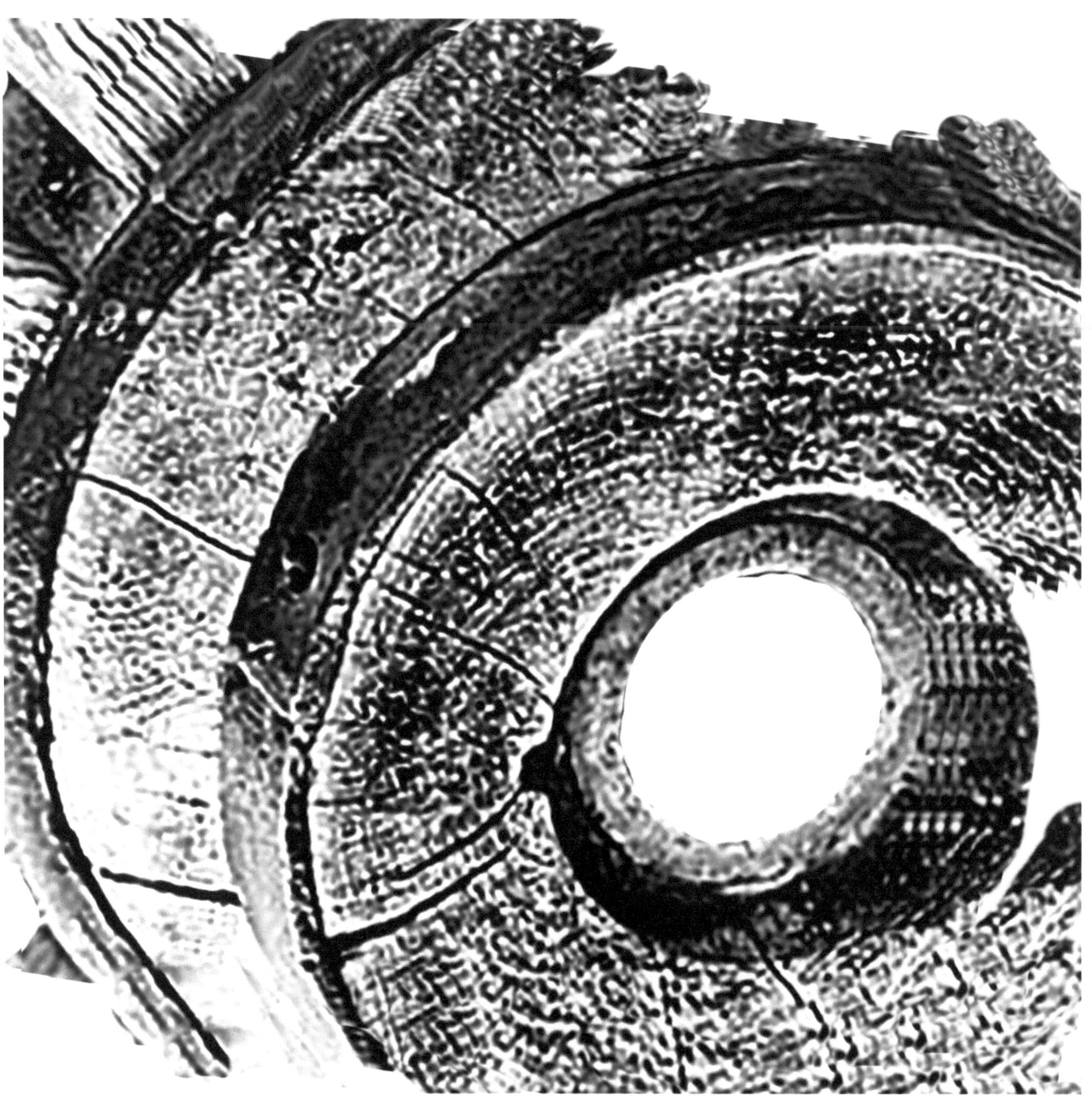

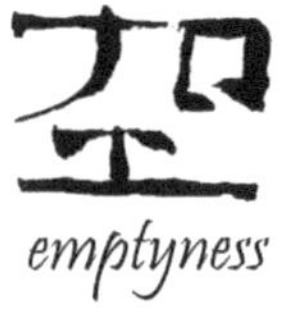

emptyness

Behold the hub.

Where there is nothing
we find the usefulness of the wheel.

Lao Tzu
Tao Te Ching

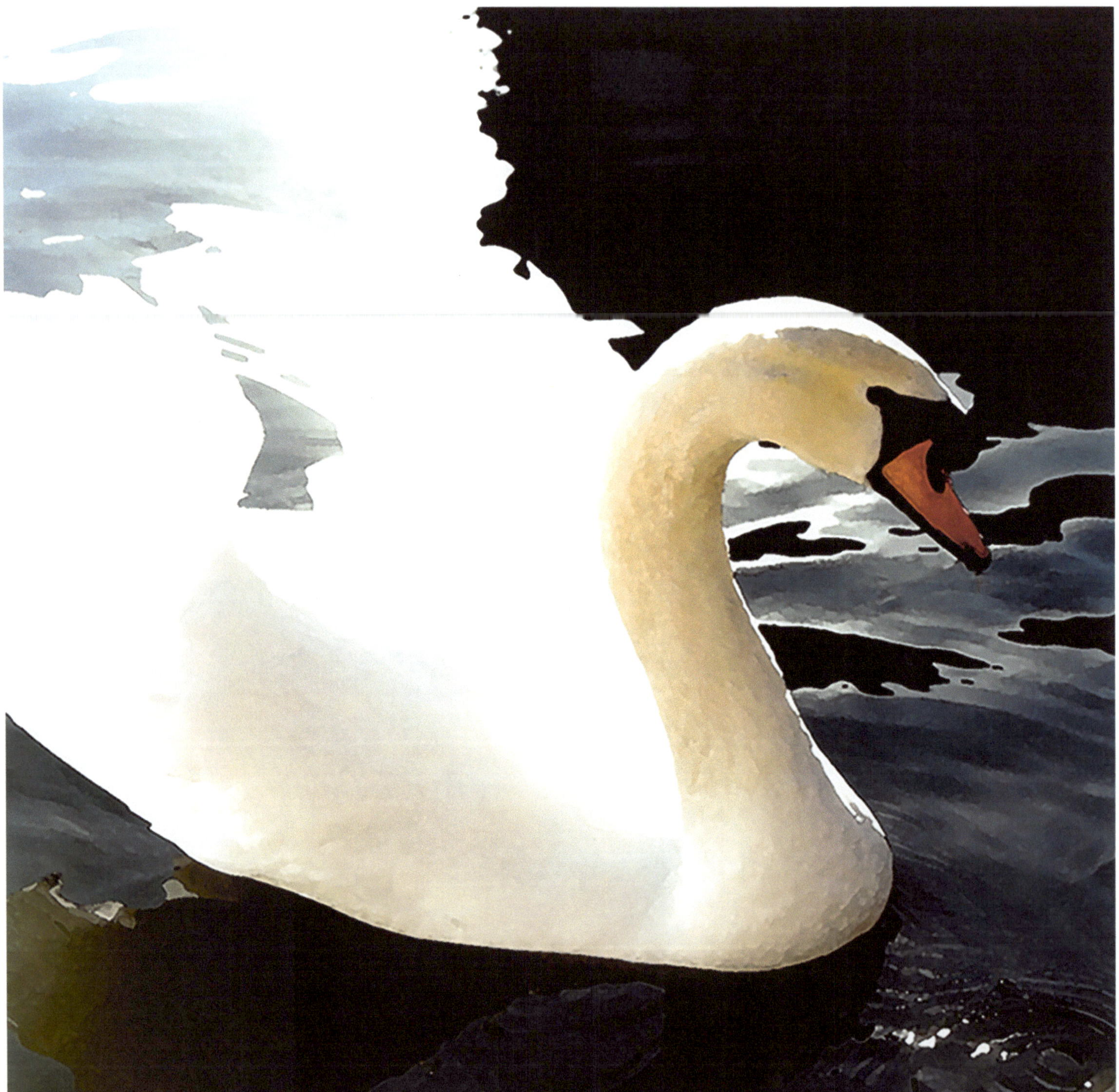

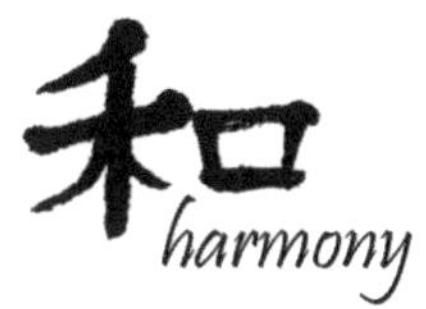

Two Views of Happiness

Swans swimming in the pond

Warm bread baking on a cold morning

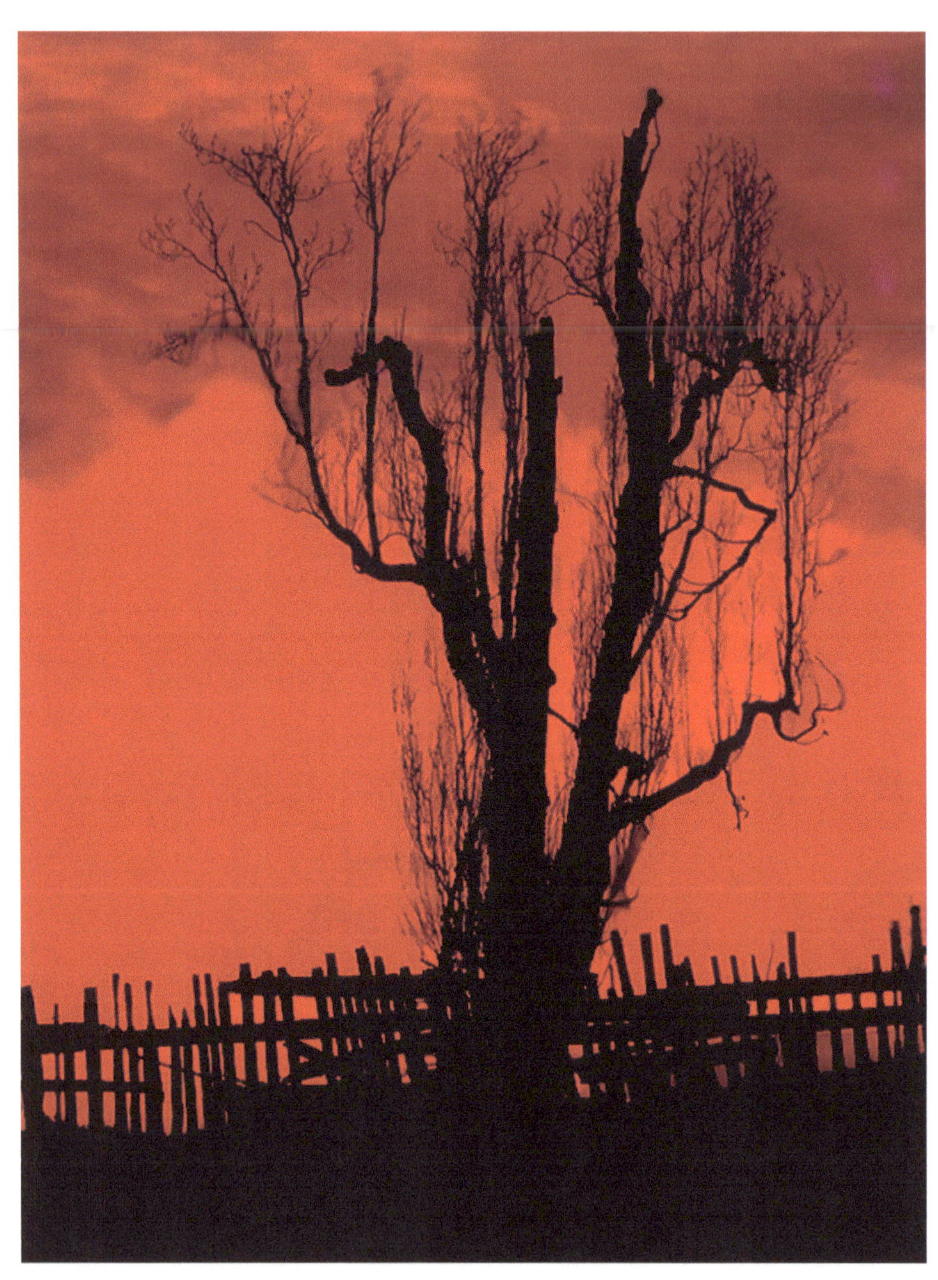

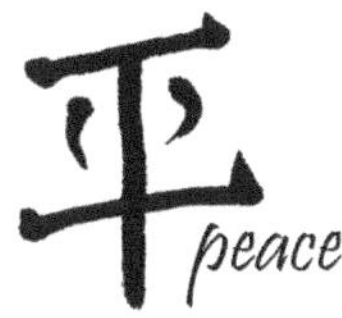

stripped trees
bone thin fired black
a cold stream echos
over the scorched woods

stumbling over a stony path
I dream of being alone
in the night's hold
with only the icy moon

once forbidding
the dark taught me
to be gentle
as the drinking deer

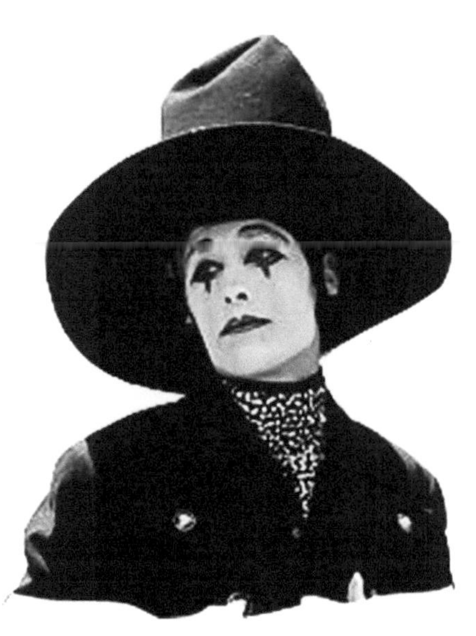

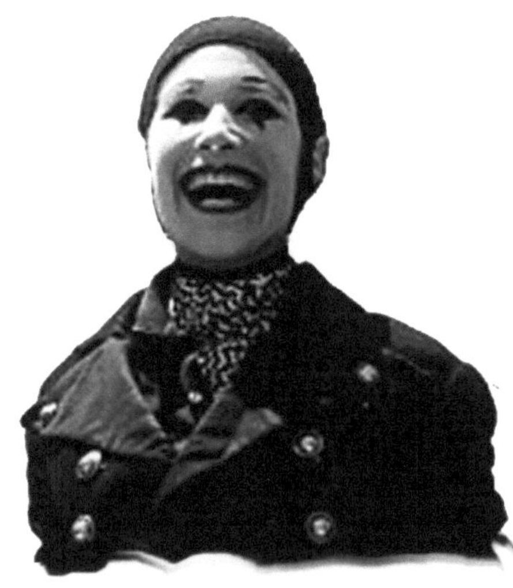

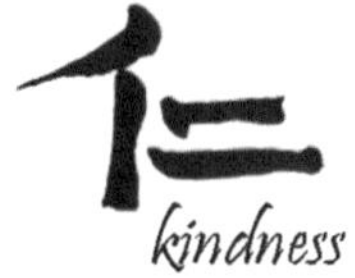

kindness

Let no one ever come to you
without leaving better, happier.
Be the living expressions of
God's kindness in your face,
kindness in your eyes, kindness
in your smile.

Mother Teresa

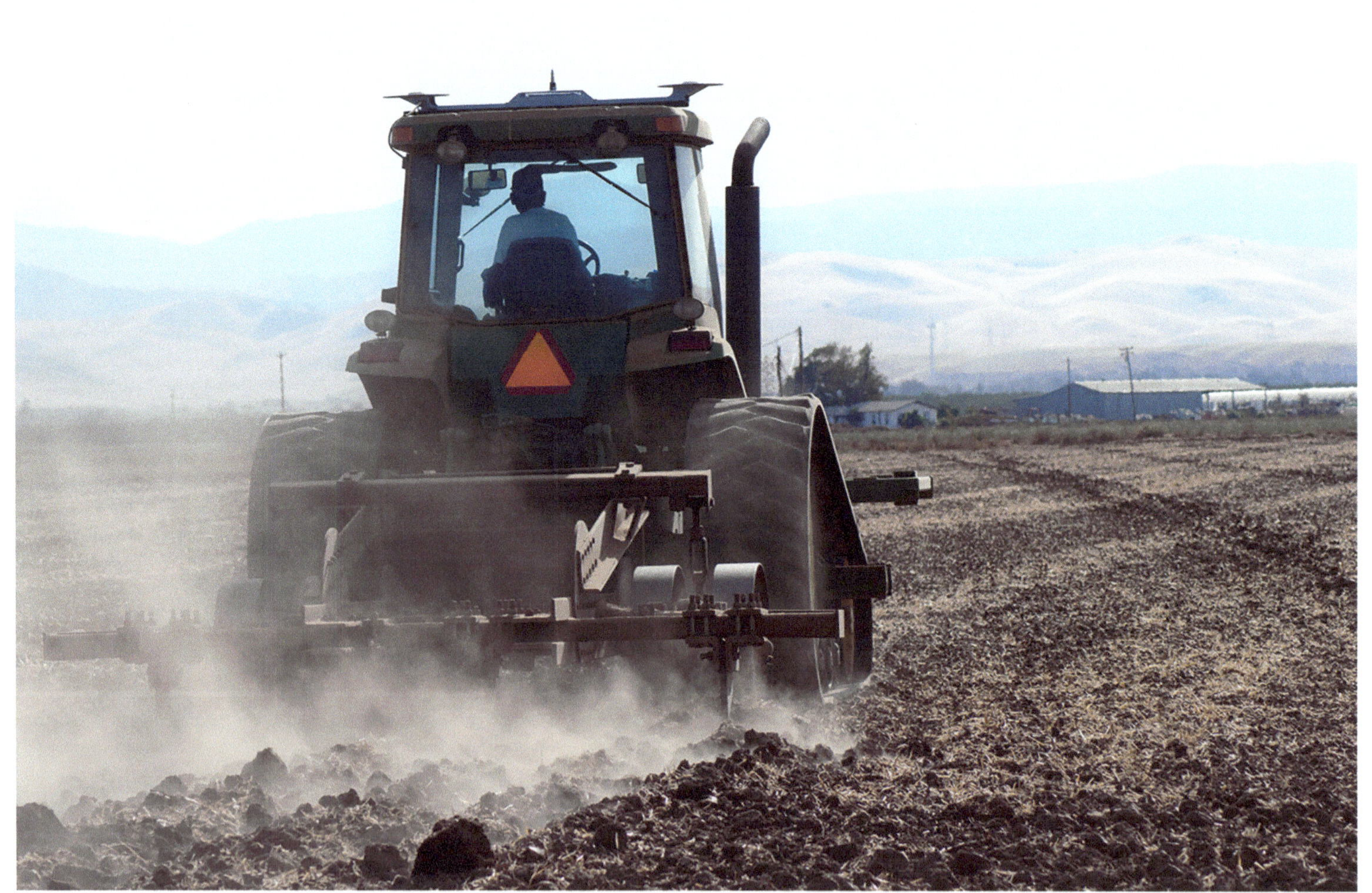

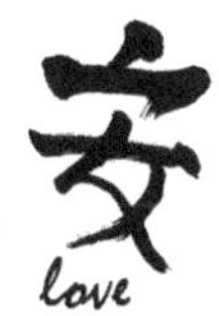

Buddah Smiles

rain and tears are one
tree and body are one
wind and breath are one

plowing the field
feeds the cranes

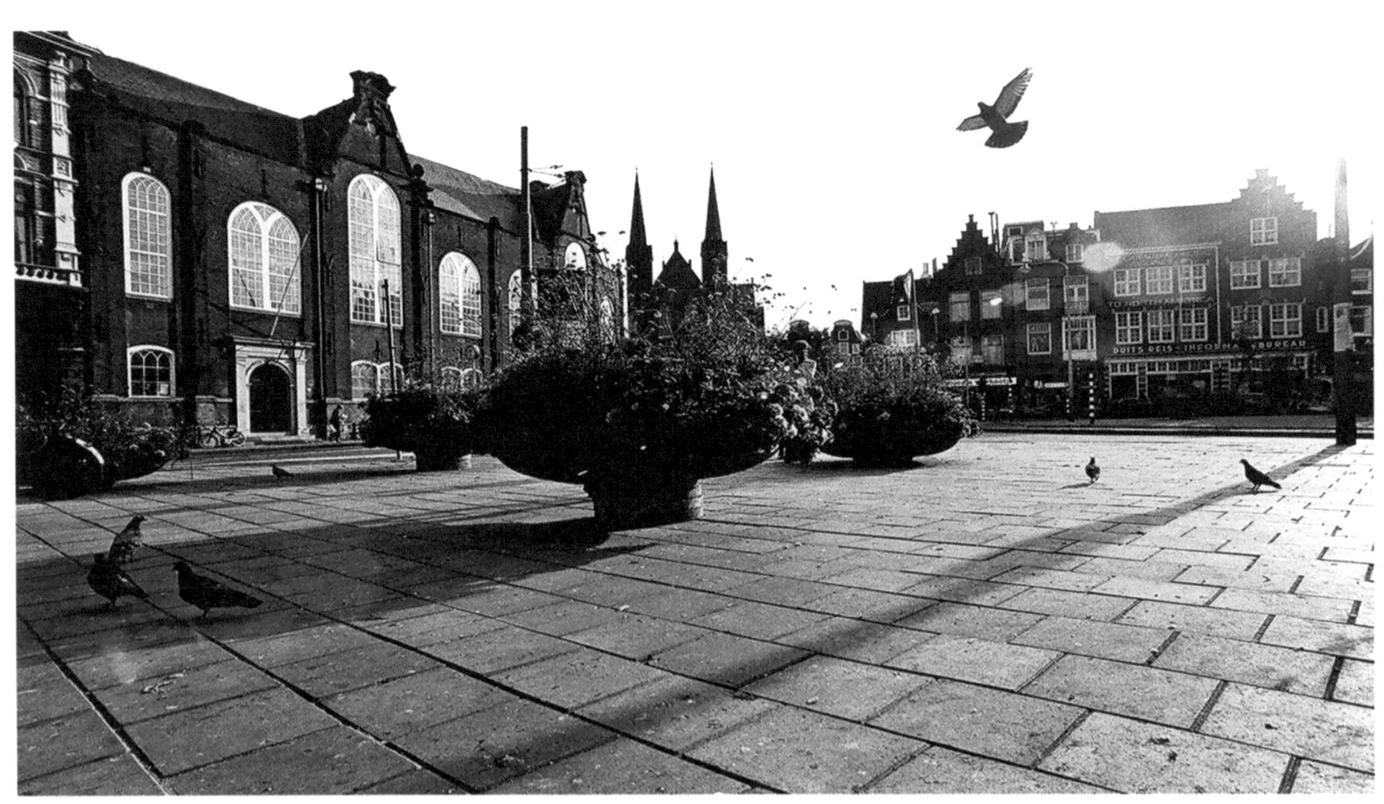

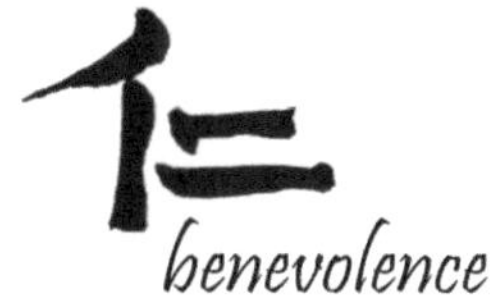

benevolence

in the light of mindfulness
every action becomes sacred
no boundary exists between
the sacred and the profane

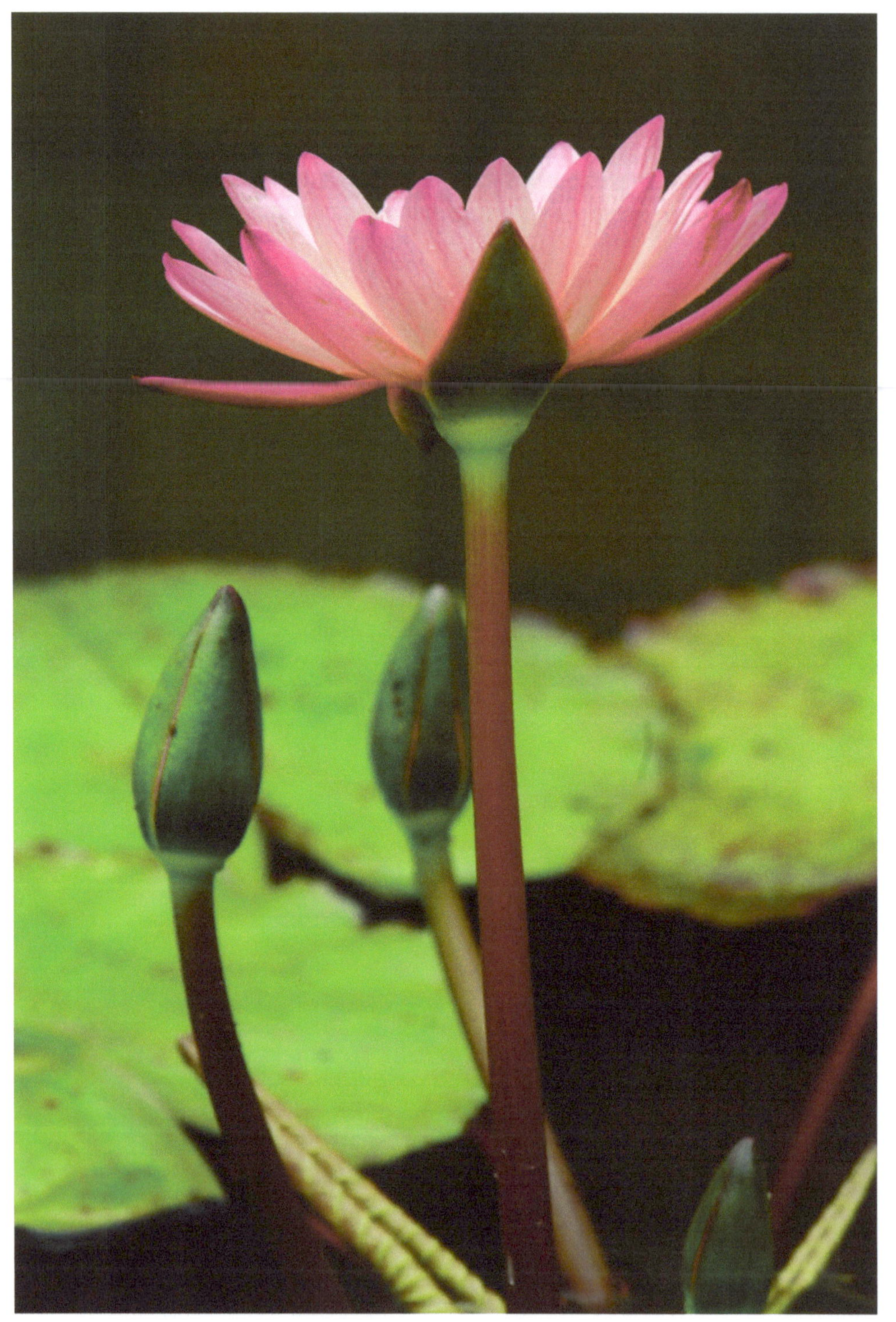

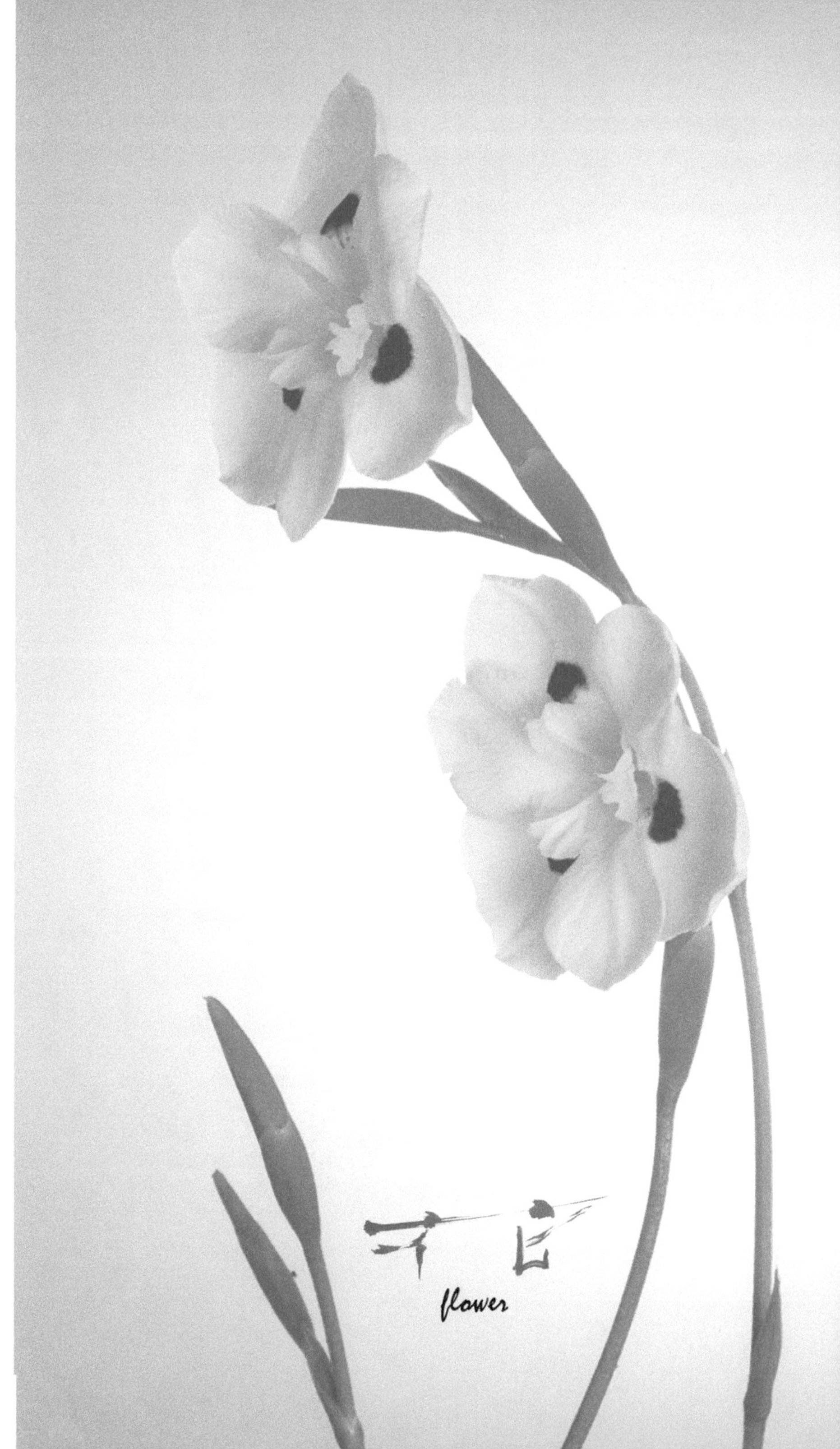

even as the gatherer
of flowers seeks to
find the finest and
rarest, so will you
gather the teachings
and transcend
this world

Buddha

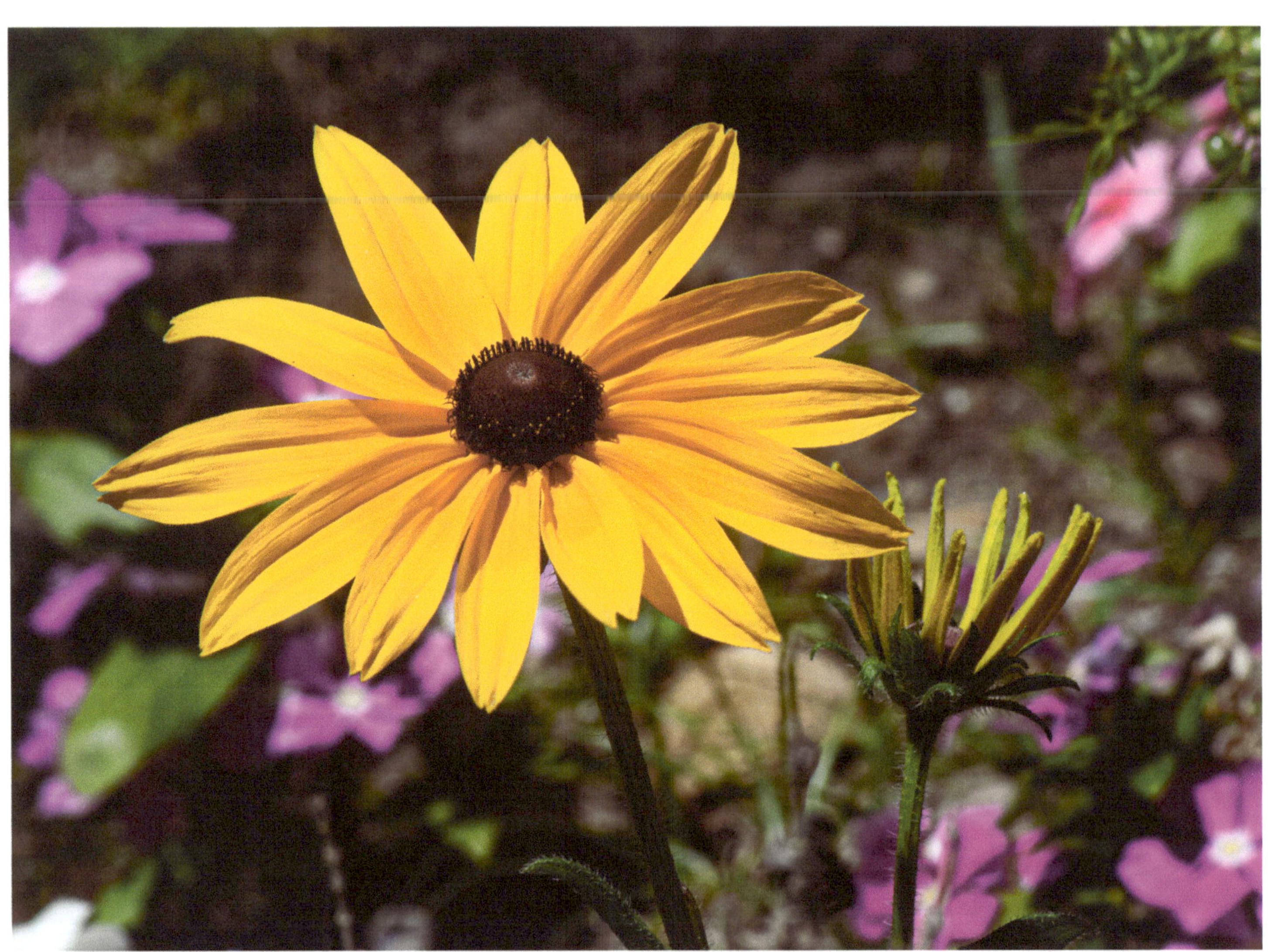

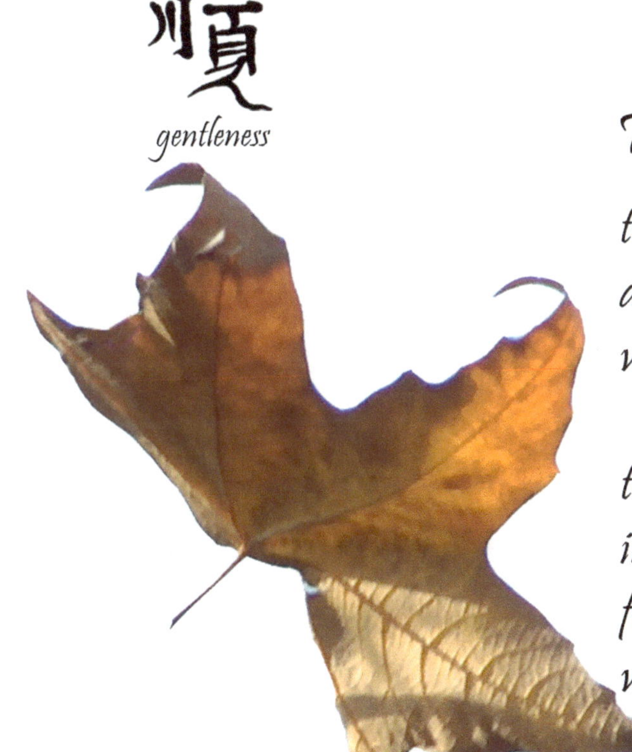

順

The Gentle Man

the leaf floats
along the running stream
without resistance

the seed swirls
in the wind
finding fertile soil
without striving

the gentle man dances
arms wide to the sky
hearing the music of light
flowing through branches

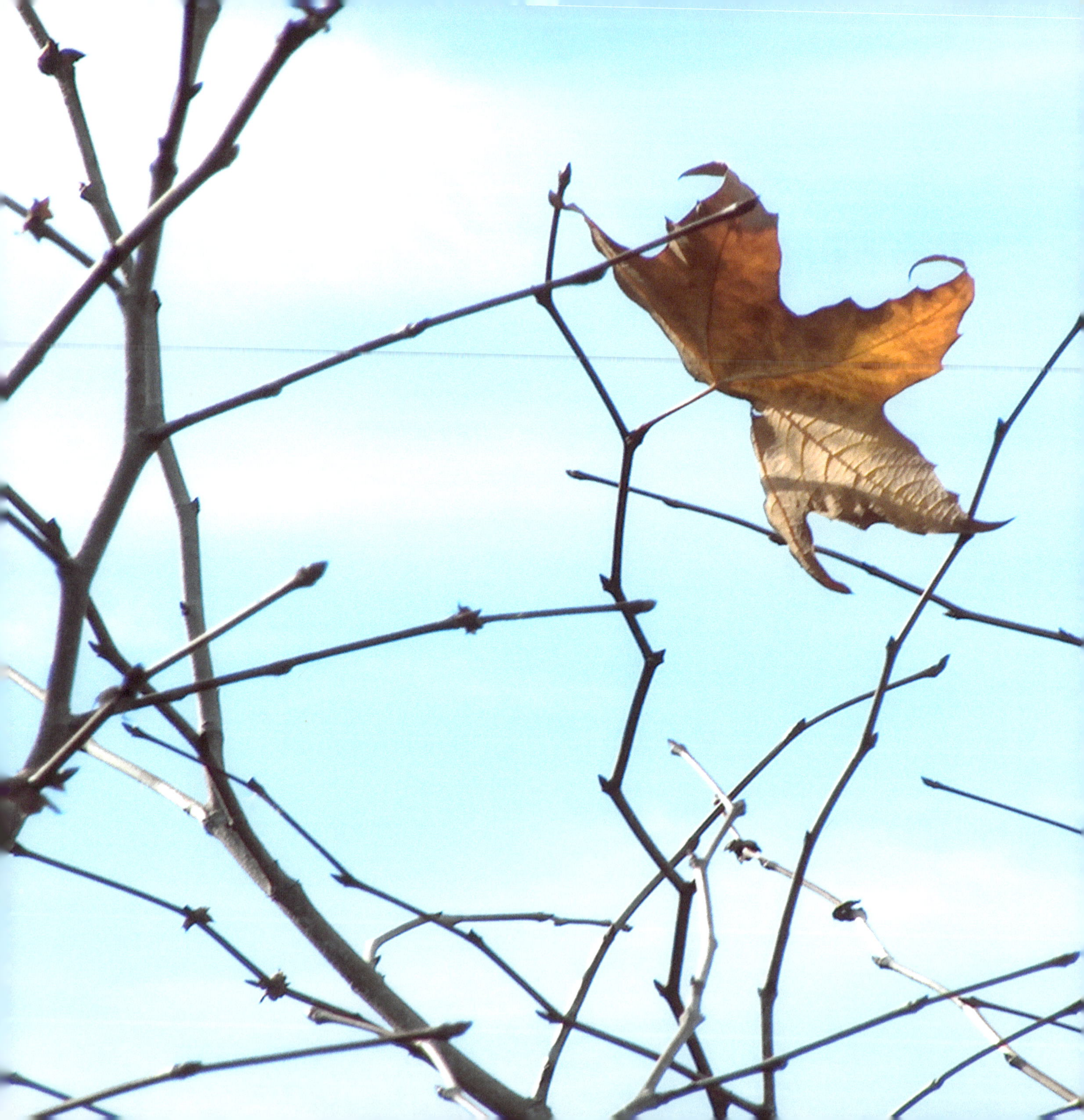

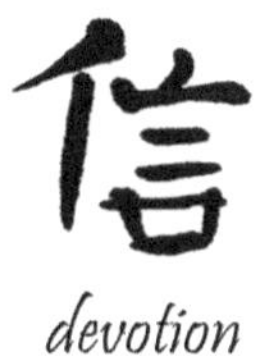

devotion

a leaf on a dying branch
young birds singing
an ancient song

thin tendrils of web

embrace a struggling moth

proud and sad

this procession of life

and death

as one

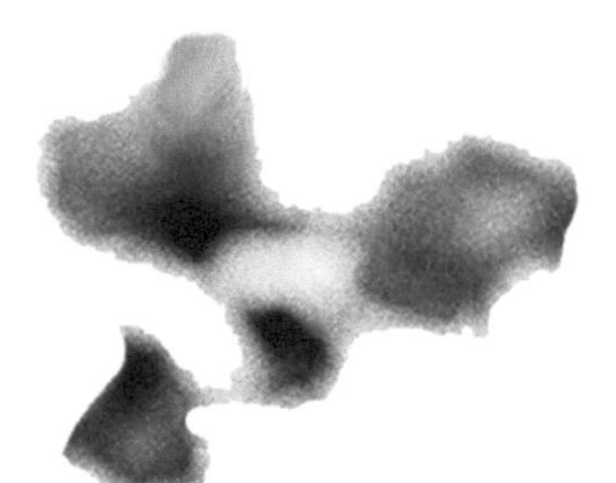

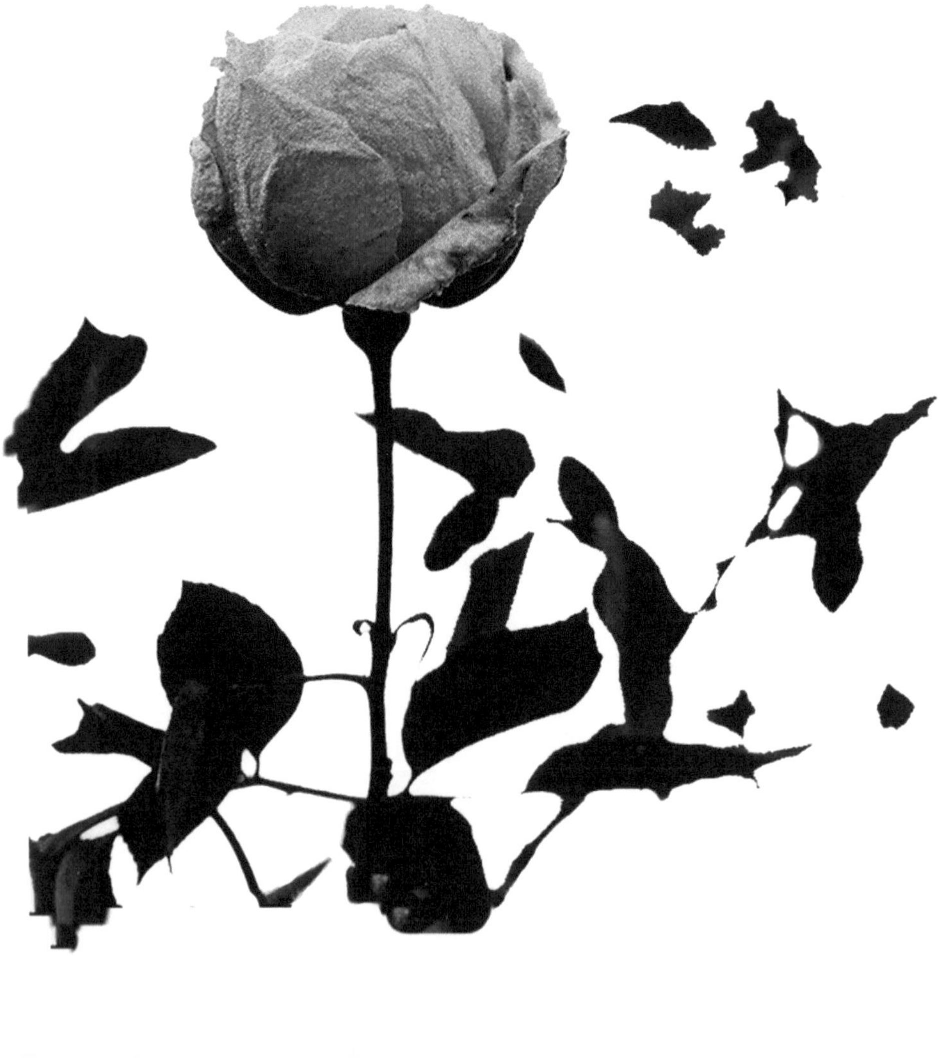

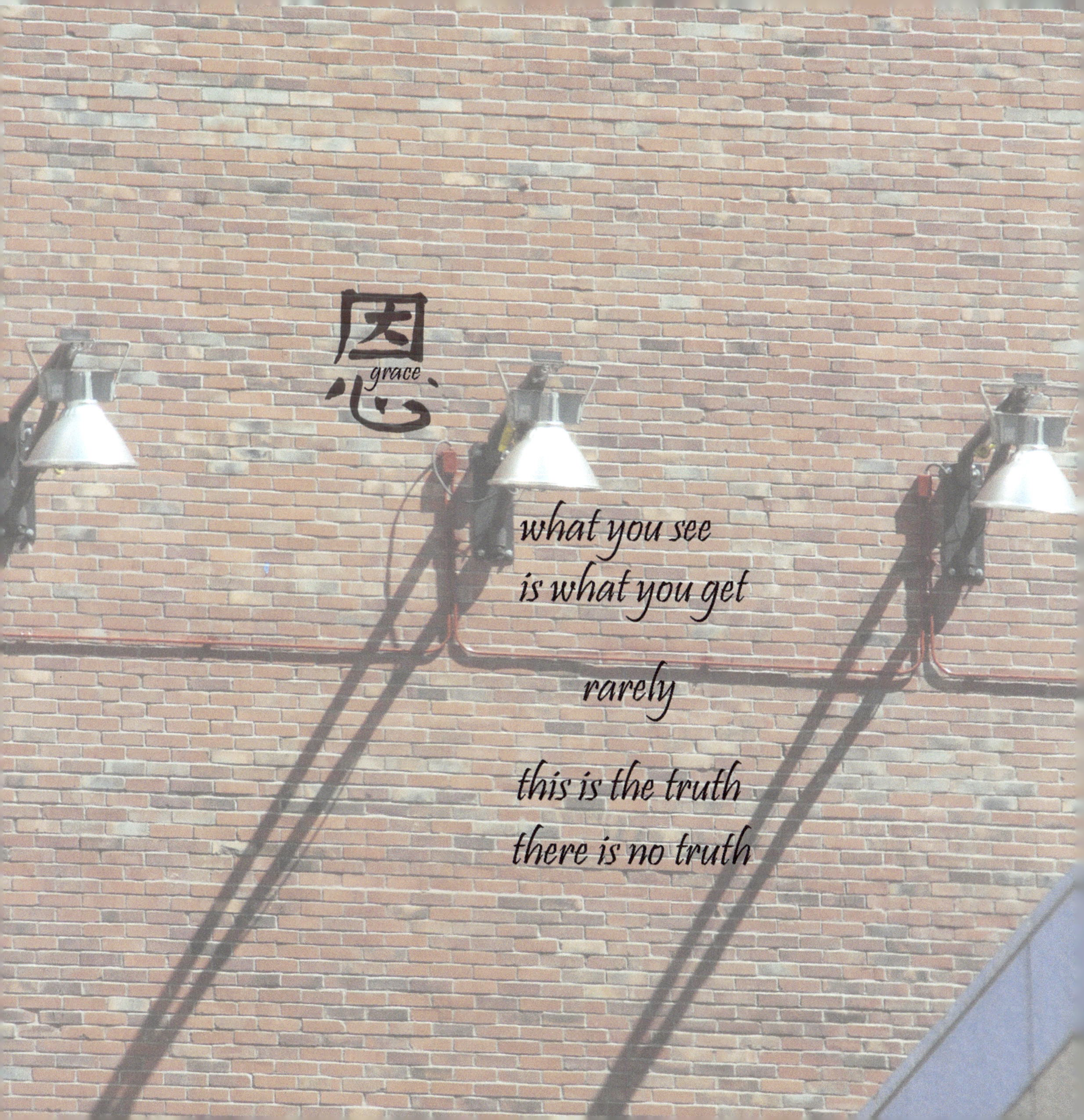
grace
what you see
is what you get

rarely

this is the truth
there is no truth

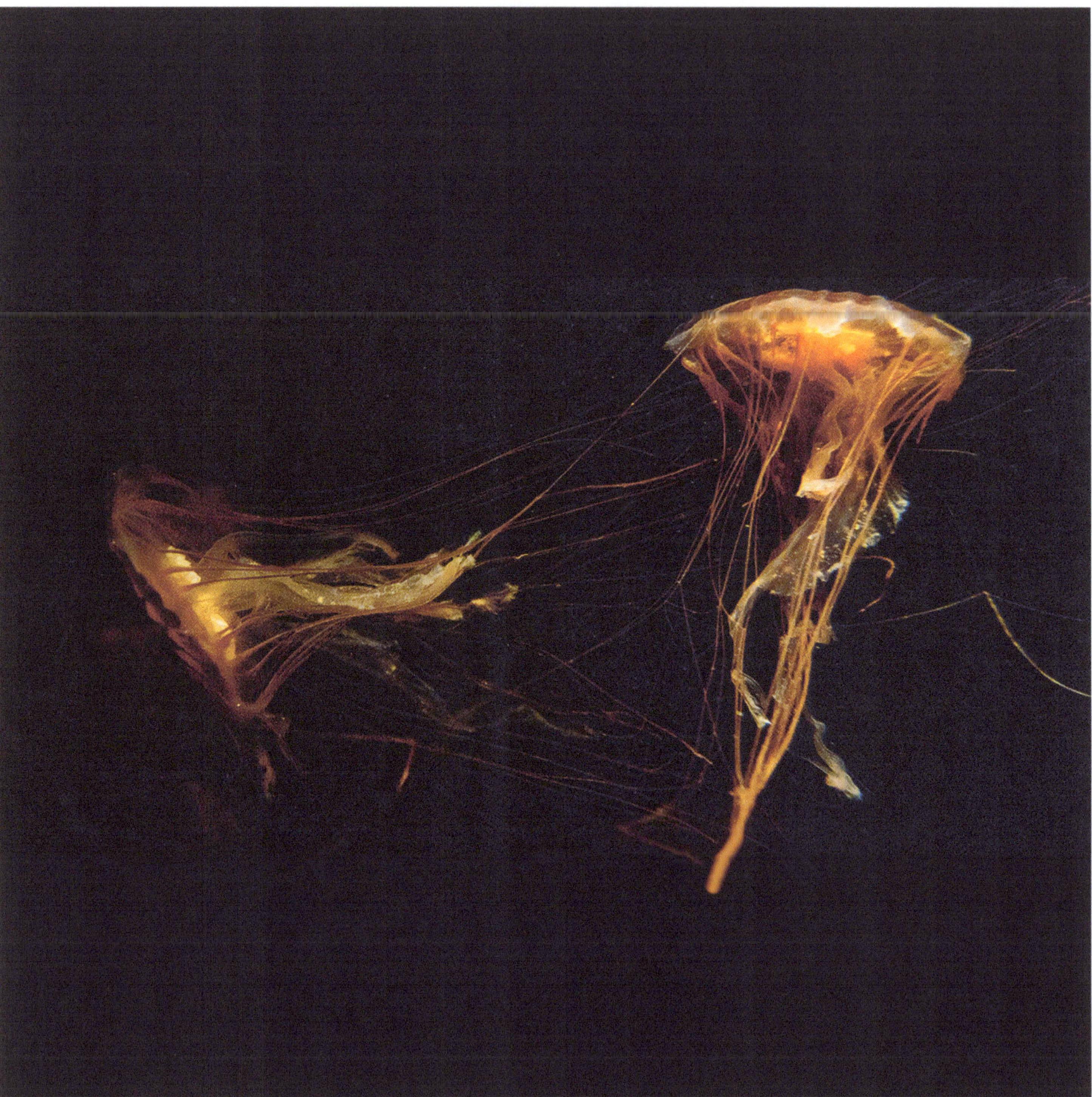

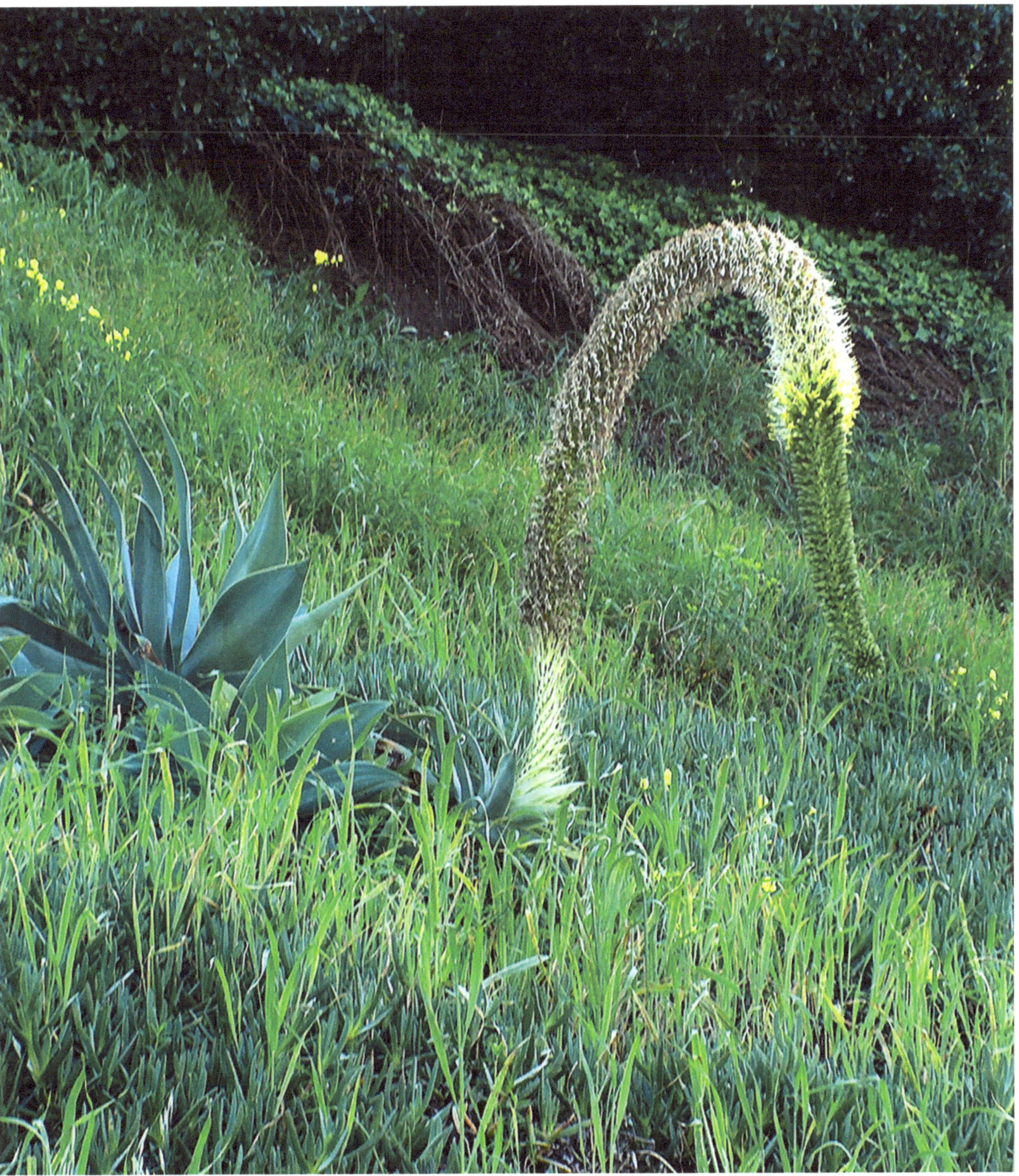

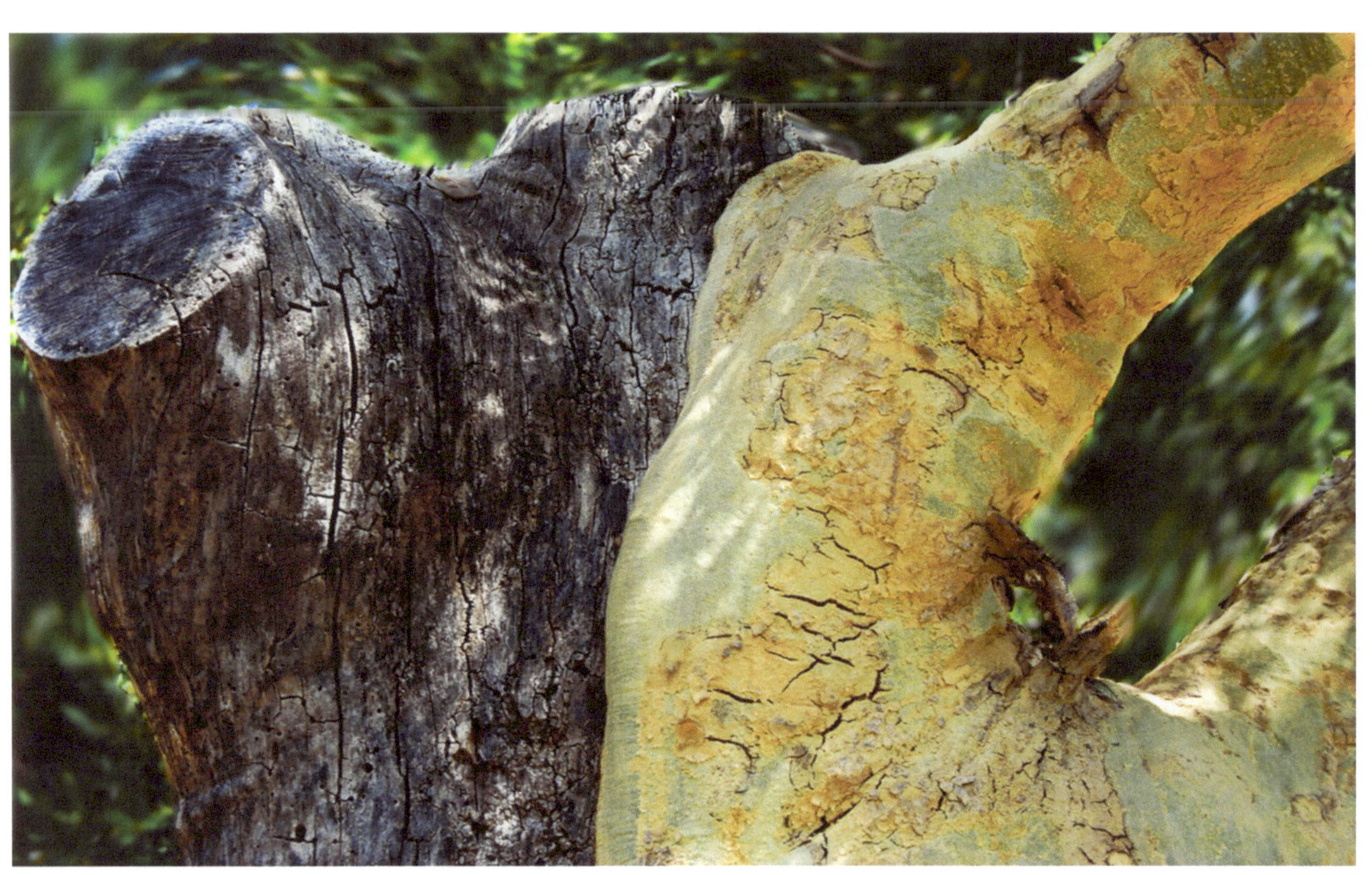

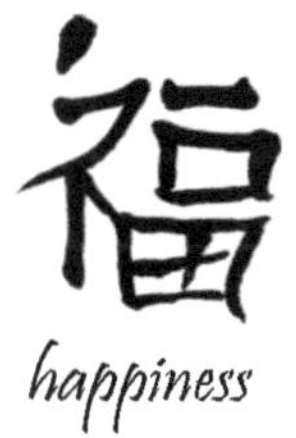

For the good of the many –
for the happiness of the many –
out of compassion for the world.

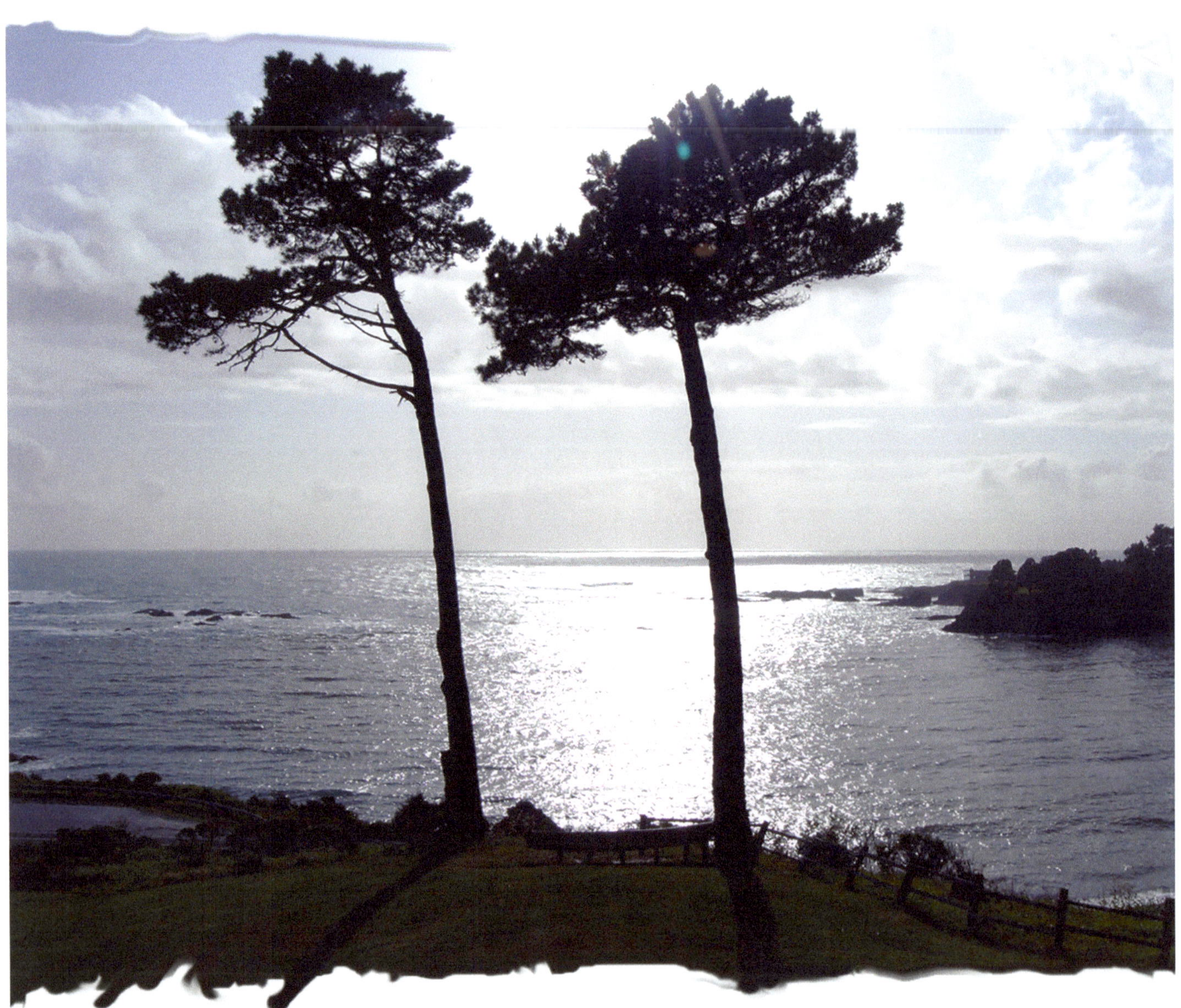

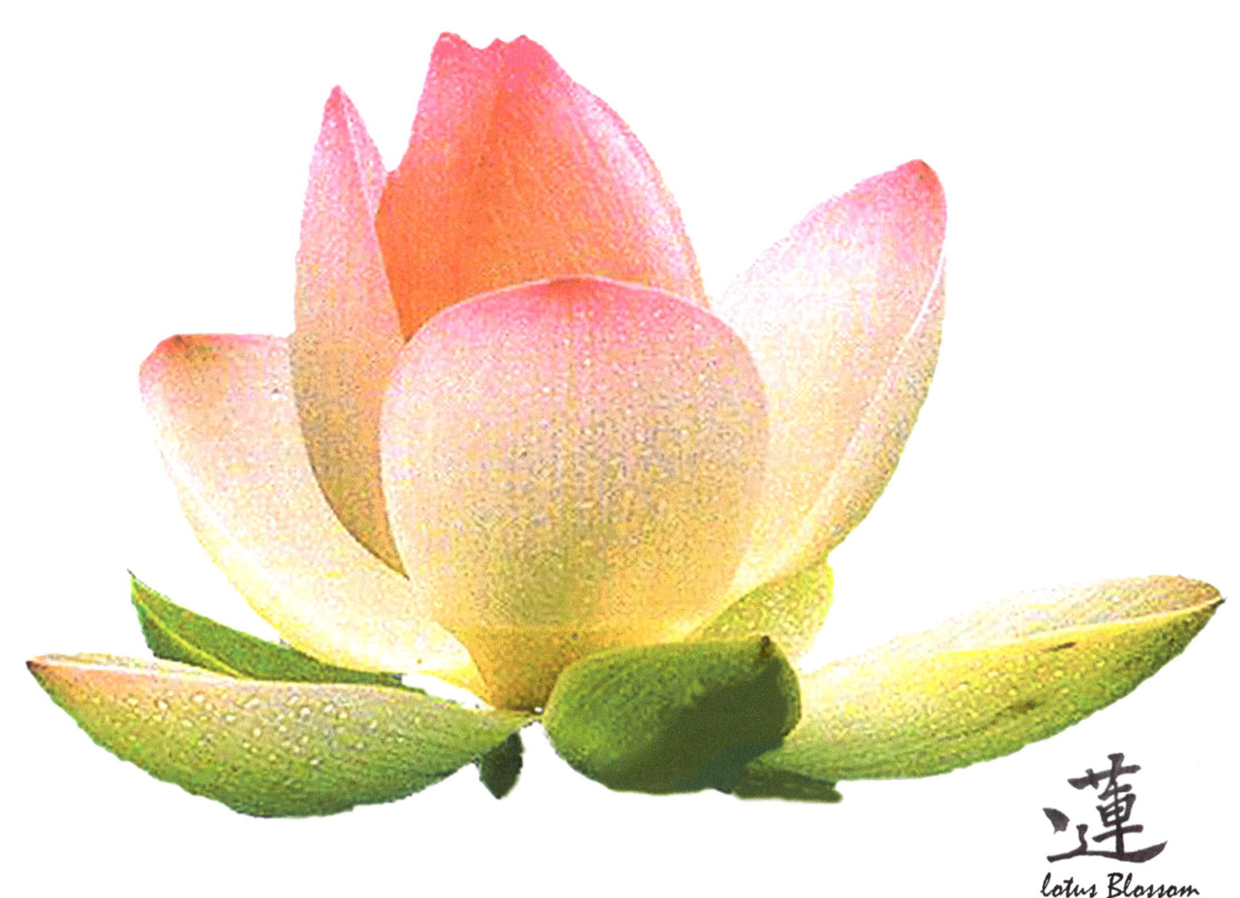

May you live like the lotus
at home in muddy waters

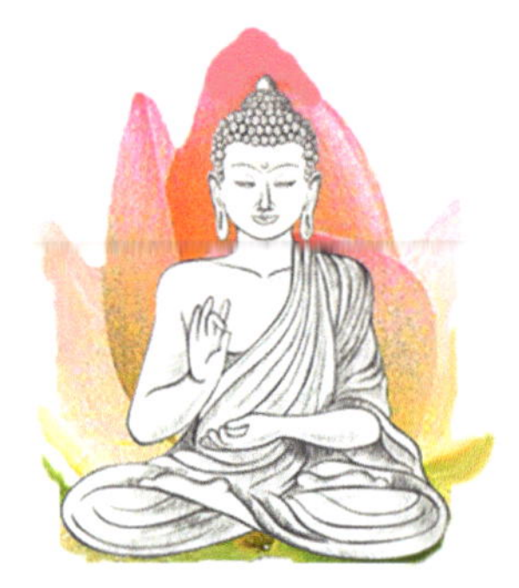

In the end, only three things
matter: how much you loved,
how gently you lived, and how
gracefully you let go of things
not meant for you.

Buddha

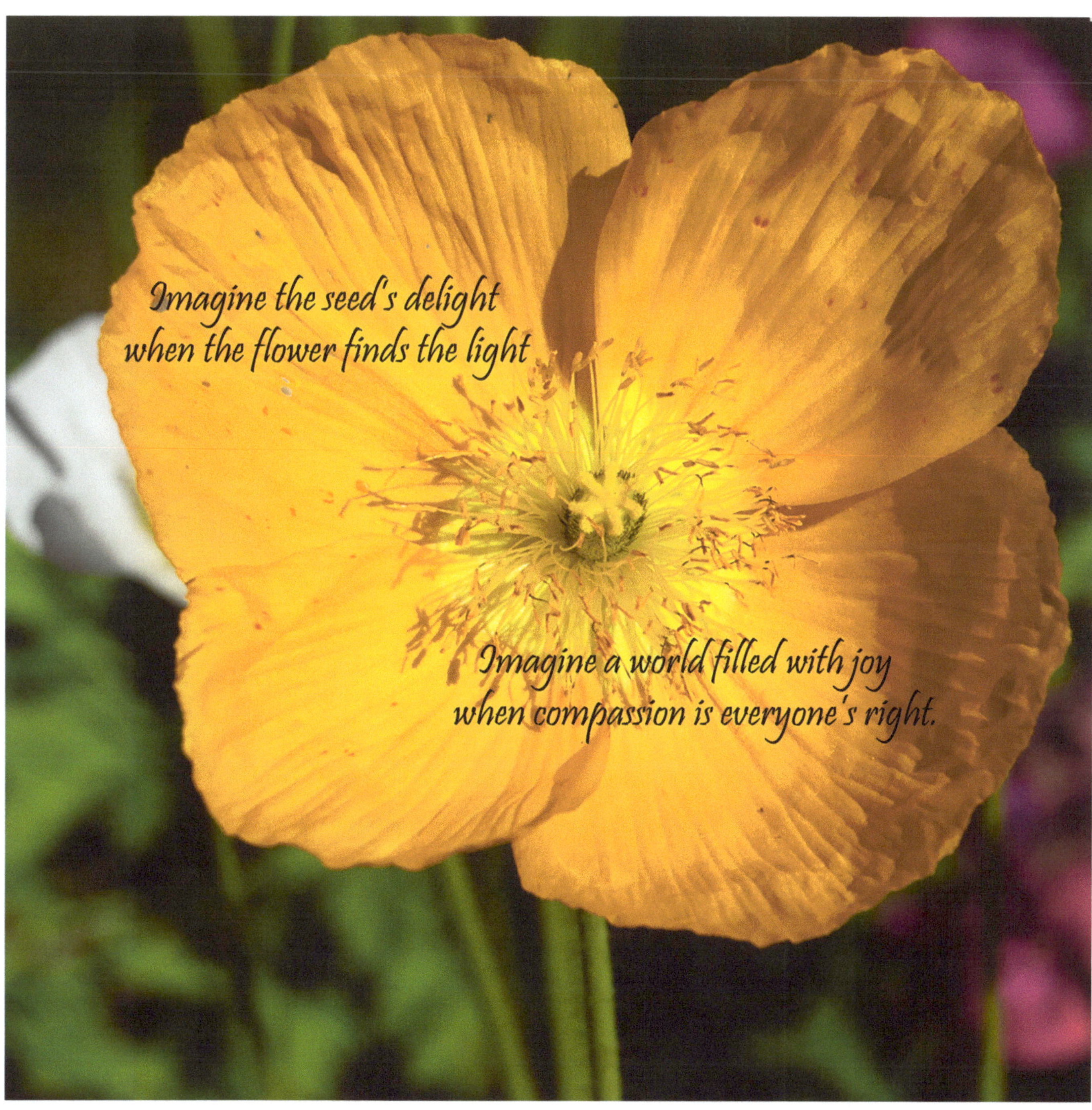
Imagine the seed's delight
when the flower finds the light

Imagine a world filled with joy
when compassion is everyone's right.

Each day I wake up and remember the words of the great teacher, Thich Nhat Hahn,
   "I'm fortunate to be alive. I have a precious human life. I am not going to
   waste it. I am going to use my energies to expand my heart to others."
That's what this small book is meant to do. Remember, as I try to, that one day
ends, another begins. As we turn towwards the crossroads upon which we meet ourselves,
instead of looking down each branch, stop and see the place in which you are. Try to
remember there is only this moment.

Remind yourself to be here, in this moment, not then, not when. Be empty, for it's
the space inside that makes a home. Be filled by living in the present, experiencing all
that surrounds you. We are not what we were. We are not what we will be. We just are.
Meet each day with compassion, with peace, with joy. Live openly, Cry with both
happiness and sadness. Laugh at yourself. Praise what is good, understand what is not
and leave judgement to history. Be thankful for the wonders you're granted, the love
given, the love gotten, friends, lessons learned. Live every day granted to you to the fullest.

                                        Allen Plone, 2022

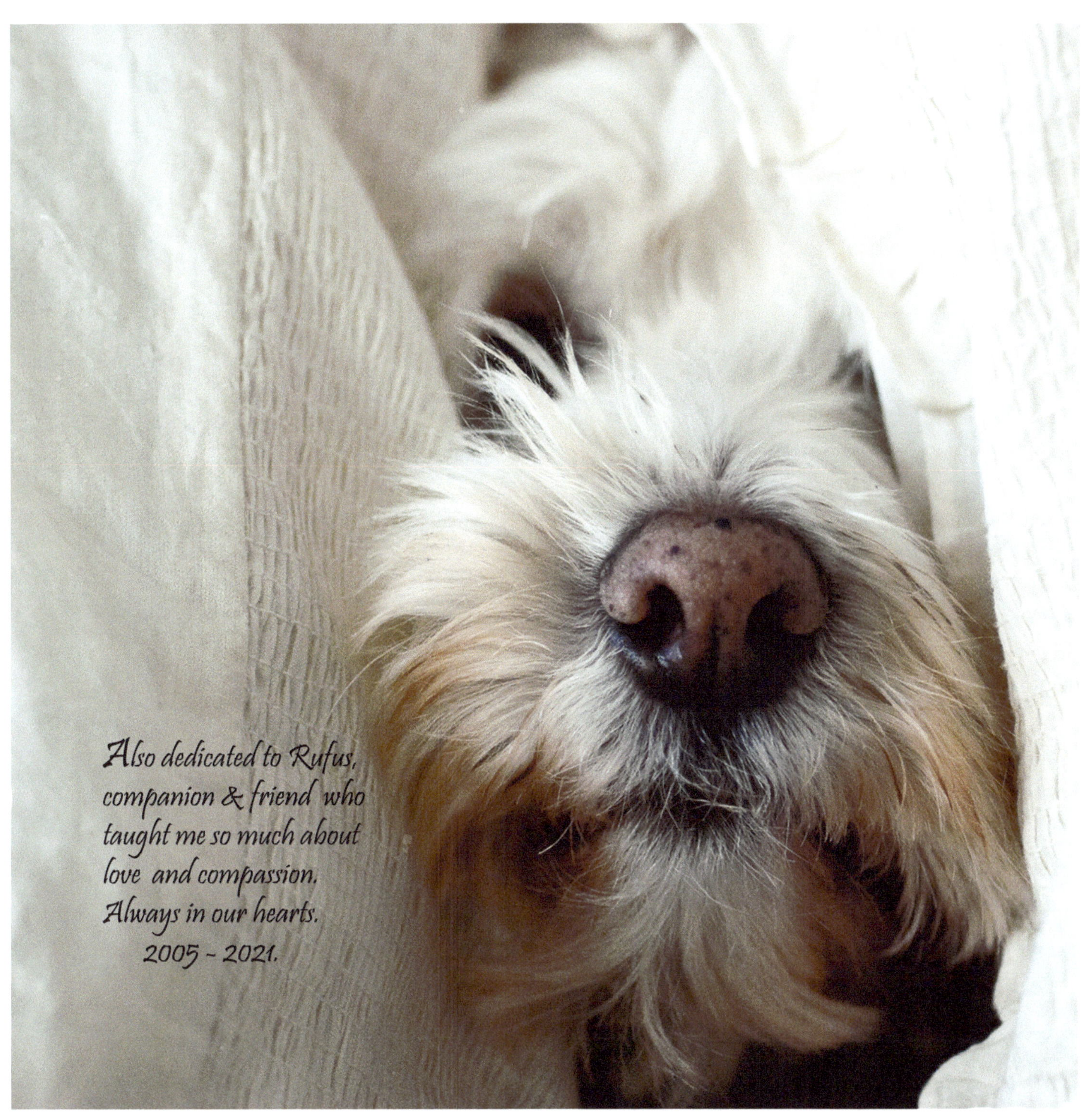
Also dedicated to Rufus,
companion & friend who
taught me so much about
love and compassion.
Always in our hearts.
2005 - 2021.

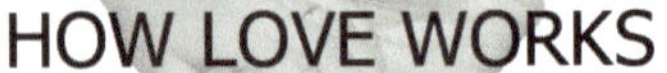

HOW LOVE WORKS

what we see of the mushroom
is less than what is there

spreading beneath its cap and stem
hyphae reach to touch entangle

each one to the next to the next
this is love when two equals one

the many together seeking
to hold onto the other

not to become the other
but to be intertwined

whispering only what needs to be said
content with the silence of touch

www.ingramcontent.com/pod-product-compliance
Lightning Source LLC
Chambersburg PA
CBHW042110030726
47599CB00002B/166